PICTURE THIS

An illustrated US History for readers with severely limited attention spans

Josh Davis

This book is dedicated to Casey Peters, Nordonia Class of 2024,
who has insisted on buying and reading my two previous books
even though I told him that they weren't appropriate for him.

Now watch; I finally write a book that I want him to read,
and he probably won't buy this one.

Please lend him your copy so he'll know that I can actually write a book
that doesn't have any expletives or inappropriate material in it.

"Who cares about
purple mountains majesty
& amber waves of grain?
The only thing that's going to
motivate me to walk
all the way to another
continent is a spa that charges
a flat fee for waxing."

Approximately 10,000-40,000 years ago,
early humans migrated from Asia to North and South America
over a period of millennia.
They traveled by foot in pursuit of large mammals that sustained
their nomadic lifestyle, and were able to cross the *Bering Strait*
from Asia to Alaska as sea levels dropped by dozens of feet
as an ice age drew water into glaciers and the polar ice cap.
It would take thousands of years but eventually humans
would populate the New World, spreading from the western
coastlines toward the interior of the newly-inhabited continents.

"Chocolate, definitely;
Ice cream, maybe;
But corn? Establishing an entire civilization based on corn?
I just don't get it."
"And that's WAY too much fiber;
The toilet hasn't even been invented yet, for God's sake."

Although tens of millions of people would come to inhabit
North and South America prior to the arrival of Europeans,
for many years most would live in small clusters
near sources of food and fresh water.
There would eventually arise substantial civilizations,
chiefly in Central America and South America,
notably the *Olmecs, Toltecs, Mayas, Aztecs & Incas*.
Cahokia near modern-day Illinois on the Mississippi River
was likely the largest civilization to flourish
in what would become the United States,
with tens of thousands of inhabitants.
For most of these large communities, it was the domestication
of *maize* (corn) that provided a consistent and reliable food
source that allowed for permanent settlements
populated by thousands of people.

"But we brought you horses, too,
so there's that ..."

Italian explorer *Christopher Columbus*, sailing west on behalf of *Ferdinand and Isabella* of *Spain*, laid claim to the "New World" in 1492, having mistakenly thought he had secured a westward route to the riches of Asia and India. Following a papal decree known as the *Treaty of Tordesillas*, Spain and Portugal would colonize and plunder great wealth from the Americas over the next several centuries. The *Columbian Exchange* references the transmission of crops, animals & diseases between Europe and the New World. It was chiefly the introduction of European diseases such as *smallpox* that would allow the colonizers to impose their rule upon the indigenous people of North & South America who lacked any resistance to the foreign illnesses, with the ravaging effects laying waste to as much as 90% of the native populations

"And you've been complaining about the occasional human sacrifice?"
"Just wait until you see what these Spanish infiltrators have planned.
Life has been a cakewalk until now."
"We'd better invent the fan because something is about to hit it."

Spain in particular flourished and became the pre-eminent world power of the 16th and 17th centuries due to the immense wealth plundered from its New World colonies. *Conquistadores* led by *Hernan Cortes* allied themselves with local tribes to topple the *Aztec* empire led by *Montezuma,* centered on the metropolis of *Tenochtitlan* in modern-day Mexico. Shortly afterwards, *Francisco Pizarro* would similarly lay waste to the *Inca* empire of modern-day Peru. Other Spanish warriors such as *DeSoto, Coronado* & *Ponce de Leon,* who would establish the first permanent European settlement in what would eventually become the United States at *St. Augustine* (Florida) would expand Spanish domination over much of the two newly-conquered continents.

"But if you don't accept Catholicism, my child, what will you do for guilt?"
"Judaism won't be here for centuries."

Via the *encomienda*, the Spanish crown granted the conquistadores control over the indigenous people in exchange for converting the native population to Catholicism. Jesuit priests established a series of missions throughout Spanish-claimed lands, justifying the subjugation and exploitation of millions in pursuit of silver and gold. ***Bartolome de Las Casas*** was a leading Spanish cleric who sought better treatment for the exploited indigenous population, helping to persuade the king to reform the encomienda, although the *asiento* system would legitimize the importation of millions of African slaves who would for centuries be condemned to servitude on behalf of their European oppressors.

"I know, I know;
nobody likes leftovers,
but I'm sure the Spaniards left something worthwhile…"
"Let's just take a look; it's not like sailing several thousand miles
over a period of months with no reliable source of food or fresh water
or communication with anyone we know is that big of a deal, right?"

While Spain & Portugal dominated the New World
to the west and south, rival European nations such as
England, France, the Netherlands and Sweden also sought both
a *Northwest Passage* to Asia as well as colonies and the riches
they could provide in the New World.
Giovanni da Verrazano sailed the east coast of North America
on behalf of *France*, and *Jacques Cartier* would claim
the *St. Lawrence River*
granting France access to the interior of North America.
Henry Hudson would lay claim to what would ultimately
become *New York* as a Dutch colony, while *John Cabot*
plied the Atlantic coast of North America for England.

"Yes, yes, yes...
we'll be back before you even know
we've left."
"You do know how to forage and
live off the land, don't you?"
"Oh, never mind;
what could go wrong?"

Seeking a base in the New World from which to plunder
Spanish galleons of their riches, *Sir Walter Raleigh*, an English
privateer sailing under the auspices of *Queen Elizabeth I*
of England established a settlement at *Roanoke Island*
off the coast of modern-day North Carolina in 1587.
Vessels intended to resupply Roanoke were delayed when the
Spanish Armada attempted to invade England in 1588,
and when English ships were finally able to return,
they found Roanoke abandoned and lifeless,
with only the word *"croatoan,"* the name of a local
indigenous tribe, carved as a clue as to what might have
happened to the first permanent English settlement
in the New World.

"Seriously?"

"We give you Pocahontas and you give us trinkets and measles?"

"If you clowns didn't have guns,

we would be having an altogether different conversation, whitey."

England's first enduring settlement would be *Jamestown*, located on the *Chesapeake Bay*. Established by the *Virginia Company of London*, a *joint-stock company* made up of investors hoping to find gold and silver, Jamestown struggled through privation and hardship after being settled in *1607*.

Under the leadership of *John Smith* and with great assistance from the local *Wampanoag* tribe, Jamestown would eventually succeed thanks largely to the effort of *John Rolfe*, who planted contraband Spanish tobacco seeds beneath Jamestown's fertile soil.

Tobacco would eventually establish itself as the region's first crucial resource, encouraging other settlers to immigrate, many via the *headright* system in which 50 acres of land was granted to anyone sponsoring someone's voyage in exchange for a period of *indentured servitude* of 4-7 years.

There's nothing funny about slavery.

In *1619*, approximately two dozen African slaves captured from
a Portuguese ship by English pirates would arrive in
Jamestown and be exchanged for supplies, bringing the first
Americans of African ancestry to the New World.
The dreaded *"Middle Passage"* would ensnare
millions of Africans into bondage, with over 400,000 eventually
being transported to what would become the United States,
a captive population that would eventually grow to 4,000,000
by the time of the American Civil War
that resulted in their freedom.
As many as a quarter of the captive men and women would die
en route in one of the great human tragedies of the modern era.

White? ✓

Male? ✓

Adult? ✓

Christian? ✓

Property-holder? ✓

"Well, shoot, c'mon in;
You're exactly what we're looking for
in the House of Burgesses."

1619 would also see the establishment of the
Virginia House of Burgesses,
the first representative legislature in what would become
the United States.
While this was indeed a small step toward a government
of, by, and for the people,
the overwhelming majority of Virginians had
no formal voice in their own governance.

"This isn't going to work out well for me, is it?"

In 1608, *Samuel de Champlain* would establish
the French settlement at *Quebec*, from which the French
would gain access to the Great Lakes
and the interior of North America.
France's settlement would be sparse,
as after the *Edict of Nantes* was implemented in 1588,
there was no impetus for the French Protestants known as
Huegenots to flee France in pursuit of religious freedom.
The French colonial presence in North America would consist
largely of traders engaged in the lucrative
trapping of beaver and other animals
and of Catholic missionaries eager to save souls.

"And, finally,
God bless us for not understanding the concept of irony,
so that our pursuit of religious freedom that has brought us
to this great land will never be tarnished by the realization
that we reject anyone else's right to worship in the manner of their choosing."
"Amen; let's eat!"

In 1620, the *Mayflower* brought several dozen *Pilgrims* to *Plymouth*, 600 miles north of Jamestown. These Pilgrims were *Separatists* from the Church of England who were persecuted for their resistance to the church and their belief that the Anglican church was not sufficiently removed from Catholic rituals. *Miles Standish* and Governor *William Bradford* would lead the Pilgrims in the establishment of the colony in which they could worship according to their faith, and sustain themselves through fishing, trapping and lumber. Plymouth further differed from Jamestown in that women and children were present from its inception, and because the Pilgrims had no intention of returning to England having made their fortunes. Prior to landing, the Puritans on board the Mayflower would agree to the *Mayflower Compact*, which is regarded as the first colonial pledge guaranteeing majority rule based on the consensus of the majority of adult, Separatist males.

"Be sure to keep a look out;
There's a good chance that
someone, somewhere
might be having a good time."

Following shortly on the heels of the Pilgrims
were the *Puritans*, a group of slightly-less zealous
English Protestants who believed
that the Anglican Church could still be reformed
and didn't need to be abandoned altogether.
Facing increasing religious persecution following the ascension
of Charles I to England's throne in 1625, approximately
1,000 Puritans led by *John Winthrop* established *Boston*
in the colony granted by royal charter to
the Massachusetts Bay Company.
Several thousand more Puritans would emigrate from England
in what would come to be known as the *Great Migration*,
establishing a thriving colony based upon fishing, whaling,
lumber & small-scale farming.
The *"Puritan Work Ethic"* would strongly influence the
nature of the region over the next several centuries,
and Winthrop's *"shining city on a hill"*
would play a leading role in colonial and early US history.

"I had 12 pregnancies,
and you think a trial is going
to be more than I can handle?"
"Banishment, smanishment;
I was going to
leave anyway."

During the 1630's, Puritan dissidents including
Roger Williams, Anne Hutchinson & Thomas Hooker
would leave the Massachusetts Bay Colony in pursuit
of greater tolerance of religious diversity.
Williams established *Providence*, which respected the
indigenous tribes of New England and tolerated members of
different faiths such as Catholics, Jews & Quakers.
Hutchinson was tried and banished from Boston for having
advocated *antinomianism*, a creed that valued faith alone over
adherence to church doctrine. Hutchinson would help
in establishing *Portsmouth*, which would join with
Providence to create *Rhode Island*. Hooker established
Hartford, which with the adoption of the
Fundamental Orders of Connecticut,
the first written constitution in the English colonies,
authorized a legislature elected by the people and
a governor elected from that legislature.

"I think we'll be okay;
just keep your eyes peeled for any farmhouses
spiraling out of the sky and a little girl with a dog…"

In 1692-93, over 200 residents of Salem Massachusetts
were put on trial for practicing witchcraft.
The initial blame was levied on *Tituba*,
a slave accused of consorting with the devil.
Mass hysteria ensued, possibly influenced by the presence
of *ergot*, a fungus with hallucinogenic properties that was
found in rye grain being stored in Salem.
By the time better judgment prevailed,
19 members of the community
and two dogs had been executed.

"There won't be Indian losses this severe until
baseball finally gets invented."

From 1643-1684 Plymouth, the Massachusetts Bay Colony, Connecticut & New Haven formed an alliance known as the *New England Confederation*.

Established to encourage mutual assistance against outside threats while England was concerned with its own Civil War, the New England Confederation is the first example of formal cooperation between English colonies in the New World. Between 1675-76, the Confederation would wage a successful war against local tribes including the Wampanoag, the Pequots, and the Mohicans organized by *Metacom* (King Philip.) *King Philip's War* would be the bloodiest war per capita in the history of what would become the United States, and marked the end of meaningful native resistance to European settlers in New England.

The *Dominion of New England* would similarly unite not only the New England colonies, but New York as well from 1686-1689 as England attempted to reassert royal control over the increasingly restive colonies and their trade with other nations. *Sir Edmund Andros*, the harsh and unpopular royal governor, was ousted when James II was swept from England's throne in *the Glorious Revolution.*

"I think we're going to need a bigger boat…"

Given its short growing season and rocky soil,
the economy of the New England colonies became dependent
on their access to water.
Almost inconceivably abundant fisheries made for a lucrative
trade in *cod*, which when salted could provide a significant
non-perishable source of protein.
Whaling was an incredibly risky but important pursuit which
provide not only food, but most significantly
whale oil which would be used for illumination.
Ship-building and *commerce*, including the slave trade
also sustained the economies of the New England colonies,
and as the industrial age would arrive, the numerous rivers
of New England would provide a source of power
for the nation's earliest factories.

"The most progressive, kind & productive
of all the colonists
and all we're going to be remembered for is
@!*% oatmeal?"
"If I weren't a pacifist,
I would be really steamed about this."

The *Middle Colonies* of New York, New Jersey,
Delaware & Pennsylvania would be settled by a more diverse
and less religiously zealous group of immigrants.
The milder climate, fertile soil and rolling countryside
would facilitate larger farms, while rivers and streams
provided a means of getting goods to market.
Welcomed by proprietor *William Penn*, the *Quakers,*
a largely-German group of immigrants who emphasized
peaceful relations with the Native Americans and who
welcomed others of diverse backgrounds made
the Middle Colonies the most diverse part of
the Atlantic seaboard,
both economically and demographically.

And down South,
the farmers were,
as usual,
keeping it classy.

Thankfully,
the lucrative
cancer-causing crop
also required
the use of slave labor,
so there's that.

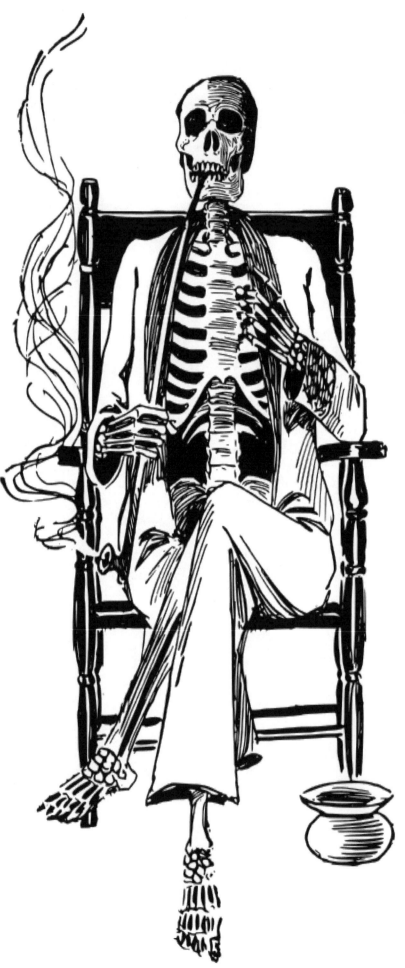

The society and economy of the southern colonies were
inextricably enmeshed with *slavery.*
Tobacco, indigo, rice & eventually *cotton*
would thrive in the warm humid climate,
and the profit generated by these cash-crops would form
the foundation of the southern economy.
While slavery, to a small extent, would exist for some time
in all 13 colonies, it was only in Virginia, Maryland,
North Carolina, South Carolina & Georgia
that it would flourish.
While a majority of southern whites were subsistence farmers
in the *Piedmont* who owned few or no slaves,
the southern *Tidewater Aristocrats* would eventually hold
literally millions of other human beings in captivity,
and the practice of slavery would bring about the greatest
challenge our nation would face in the American Civil War.

"Well of course you can worship any faith you like;
You are Christian, aren't you?"

In 1634, *Cecil Calvert (Lord Baltimore)* inherited *Maryland* as a *proprietary colony*. Calvert established Maryland as a haven for Catholics, and as Protestants began to outnumber Catholics there, Calvert persuaded the legislature to adopt the *Maryland Act of Toleration* in *1649*, which granted freedom of religion to all Christians, but which still allowed for the execution of any who rejected Jesus as savior. This will stand as the first step toward a degree of religious freedom sanctioned by the government in what would eventually become the United States.

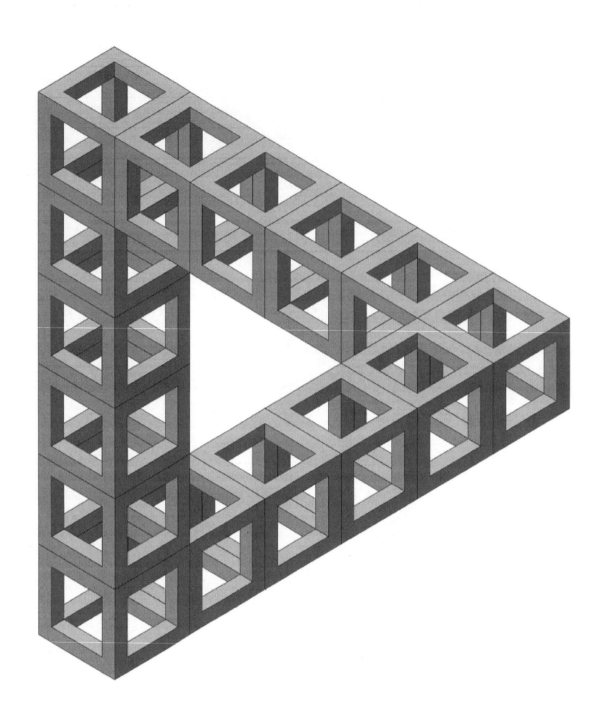

"I have a feeling that we're making this out to be slightly more complicated than is necessary ..."

The English government established the North American colonies as a source of raw materials and a market for finished goods. This type of economic system was known as *mercantilism*, and was designed for the enrichment of the mother country. England implemented restrictions on colonial trade that mandated the use of English crews on English ships with colonial commodities having to ship through England prior to being traded with other nations. A number of *Triangular Trade* routes developed in which ships would, for example, deliver slaves from Africa to the West Indies in exchange for sugar which would be distilled into rum in New England which would then be shipped back to England.

"No; it was decidedly __NOT__ followed shortly thereafter by rebellions on the parts of lettuce and tomato."

"There is clearly a need for government-funded public education."

"When are we finally going to get around to this?"

In 1676, Virginia backwoods farmers led by *Nathaniel Bacon* conducted what is regarded as the first armed insurrection against the English government. *Governor William Berkeley* had financial interests in trading with Native Americans on the frontier and interfered in the farmers' plans to roust the tribes from land in which they were interested. Due to this and rivalries between the landed gentry and their more rural peers, Bacon led a contingent of disgruntled farmers and formerly indentured servants in an attack on the colonial capital at Jamestown. The capital was burned and Berkeley forced to flee, but the uprising was eventually put down in 1677 when Bacon died of dysentery and English reinforcements suppressed what has come to be known as *Bacon's Rebellion*.

"Not rude awakening, you twit;
Great Awakening."

"And get it right;
There's going to be another."

The *Great Awakening* was an intense surge of Protestant fervor led by evangelical ministers such as **Jonathan Edwards, George Whitefield & John Wesley** that coursed through the American colonies from approximately 1730-1755. Reawakening a diminishing passion in many colonial Protestants, sermons such as Edwards' **Sinners in the Hands of an Angry God** galvanized thousands to embrace their faith wholeheartedly with every fiber of their being. The *Congregationalist, Methodist & Baptist* churches would see a surge in their popularity that would swell their numbers with new converts who feared eternal damnation should they not be "born again" and commit their lives to God. The Great Awakening would be the first of several periodic religious revivals which would course through what would become the United States.

*Just imagine the uproar there would have been
if more than a third of the population had actually been able to read!*

A blow would be struck in favor of *freedom of the press*
in 1735 when ***John Peter Zenger***,
publisher of the <u>New York Weekly Journal</u> was acquitted of
libel by a jury of his peers. According to English common law
at the time, criticism of government officials, even if truthful
and warranted, was grounds for imprisonment on the charge
of libel. Zenger accused Governor William Cosby of
corruption for rigging elections and for having given
aid & comfort to the French. Although Zenger had clearly
broken the law, the jury deemed him not guilty as the charges
were verifiably accurate. This acquittal served
as an important precedent for the continued scrutiny
of government officials and for
the *1st Amendment* guarantee of freedom of the press
enshrined in the ***Bill of Rights***.

"I know;
let's confuse generations of students by calling it
The French & Indian War
when it was fought between the French and the British
or
The Seven Years War
when it actually lasted nine."

Over the course of the 18th century, a series of four wars would be waged between the British and the French alongside various proxies. The third of these, *King George's War*, would inspire resentment on the part of colonists when the French outpost of *Louisbourg* which guarded the entrance to the St. Lawrence River was captured with the aid of colonial militias but was returned to French control in exchange for concessions in India.

Tensions would again boil over in 1754 when British forces including a Virginia militia regiment commanded by *George Washington* were defeated at *Fort Duquesne* (Pittsburgh). The French continued to hold an advantage until the ascension of British Prime Minister *William Pitt* changed the course of the war when he focused British strategy on conquering *Quebec* so as to control access to French Canada. Following a decisive battle on the *Plains of Abraham* and the taking of *Montreal*, the French withdrew from their North American colonies altogether, removing the threat posed to American colonists by the French and their allies.

"Wait a second; what?!?"
"We just fought for nine years and now
we can't go any further than
the Appalachians?"

"Usually someone at least
buys a person dinner
before they
pull a move like this."

Shortly after the *Treaty of Paris* ended
the *French & Indian War*, native forces under the leadership
of Chief *Pontiac* attacked 11 British forts on the frontier,
capturing or destroying eight of them. In an effort to contain
both the cost of military engagement and to avoid further
confrontation between settlers hungry for land that now
stretched from the Appalachian Mountains to the
Mississippi River, Parliament issued the *Proclamation of 1763*
which prohibited colonial settlement west of the mountains.
The establishment of the *Proclamation Line* in reaction to
Pontiac's Rebellion and British efforts to recoup
the costs of war and of maintaining their empire would
contribute to simmering resentment against the British which
would soon boil over with the
coming of the American revolution.

*"Yep; it's because we have no say in Parliament
that we're griping about paying taxes."
"Otherwise we'd be delighted to;
I mean, who doesn't love paying taxes to the government, right?"*

Foremost among colonial complaints was a lack of representation in Parliament. While the British claimed that all citizens were represented by all members of Parliament, a concept known as *virtual representation*, the colonists deemed their lack of a voice as inconsistent with English common law. When Prime Minister *George Grenville* ended the practice of *"salutary neglect"* with more rigorous enforcement of the *Navigation Laws* and with the passage of the *Sugar Act, Quartering Act & Stamp Act* in the 1760's, organized colonial opposition emerged. The Stamp Act required a government tax be paid on all printed materials and was the first tax paid directly by the colonists. Representatives of nine colonies met in New York in 1765 in the *Stamp Act Congress* to oppose *"taxation without representation"* with boycotts and violence carried out by the *Sons of Liberty*. In 1766 Grenville was replaced and the Stamp Act repealed, but Parliament passed the *Declaratory Act* emphasizing its right to tax the colonists as it pleased.

"Okay, so we may have gone
a little bit overboard with the tombstones,
but we're trying to make a point.
This is what happens when you have to
use free clip-art to avoid
any copyright infringement."

From 1767-1770, Parliament imposed the *Townshend Acts* which were duties on lead, glass, paper, paint & tea. The revenue from these taxes was to pay royal officials so that their salaries would no longer be dependent upon colonial legislatures, and Parliament authorized *writs of assistance* which were blanket search warrants which would allow royal authorities to search for goods smuggled to avoid payment of these duties. England would repeal all but a token tax on tea in 1770, but not before British soldiers, stationed in Boston to protect customs officials, were assaulted by a rowdy mob and subsequently opened fire, shooting 11 protesters. Among the five killed was *Crispus Attucks*, a mixed-race dockworker who is considered by many to be the first casualty of the American Revolution. This *Boston Massacre* would lead patriots such as *Samuel Adams, James Otis, Patrick Henry & John Hancock* to organize *Committees of Correspondence* through which each colony could remain apprised of concerns and coordinate action throughout colonial America.

"Seriously?"
"We already treat the Indians like crap;
now we're going to make them take the heat for this, too?"
"No wonder everyone thinks people from Boston
are wicked obnoxious."

On December 16th, 1773
a mob of drunken patriots dressed as Native Americans
boarded a ship in Boston Harbor and
dumped 342 crates of tea into the water.
The *Boston Tea Party* took place as a protest against
the Tea Act of 1773 and the monopoly granted to
the *British East India Company* to sell tea in the colonies.
Even though the taxed tea was cheaper than
smuggled alternatives, the colonists rejected
Parliament's perceived abuse of power.
Parliament's reaction would be swift and severe,
and the passage of the *Coercive Acts* would help
to precipitate the American Revolutionary War.

"This is either going to be the most extreme pedicure I've ever had, or I may have gone a bit overboard with that whole 'tea party' thing last night."
"Maybe if we had drank the tea instead of all that rum, I wouldn't be in this predicament…"

1774 would see Parliament strike back against the
upstart colonists with a series of reprisals
for their impertinence. Known in the colonies as
"the Intolerable Acts," the *Coercive Acts* suppressed the
power of the Massachusetts legislature in favor of the royal
governor, allowed for royal officials accused of crimes to be
tried in England rather than the colonies, expanded the
Quartering Act imposing regular British troops on colonial
hosts and closed Boston Harbor until the cost of the tea
destroyed in the Boston Tea Party had been repaid.
The *Quebec Act* concurrently established Quebec as a colony
without a legislature and with Catholicism as its
official religion stretching all the way from
the Atlantic seaboard to the Ohio River.

"No; it's <u>Paine</u> with an 'e.'"

The rationale for colonial independence was rooted in ideas emerging from *Enlightenment* philosophers such as *John Locke* and contemporary thinkers such as ***Thomas Paine***. Locke, in his ***Two Treatises of Government***, suggested that sovereignty ultimately resides with the people, and that God had established ***"natural laws"*** guaranteeing certain rights to all people. Locke stipulated that among these rights was an obligation to resist and replace any government that usurped these rights.

Thomas Paine published ***Common Sense*** in 1776, in which he argued that it was unjust for a small, remote, and corrupt British government to rule over a large distant population that had no say in its own governance. Paine's pamphlet would become one of the most important and widely-read documents in early United States history.

*"Okay; first things first.
What should we do about Parliament's outrages?"*

*"Then, once we've nailed that one down,
let's focus on figuring out
why we are we all dressed as though it's the early 1900's."*

In September of 1774, all of the colonies except for Georgia sent
delegates to the *1st Continental Congress* in Philadelphia
to form a plan of action in response to the Intolerable Acts.
The Congress created the *Continental Association*
to enforce a boycott of British goods
which had been implemented by Massachusetts
pending repeal of the onerous laws,
drafted a letter to the King seeking his assistance and support,
and decided to meet again in May of 1775
if the British did not redress the colonists' grievances.

"Now was it 'one if by land, two if by sea'
or the other way around?"

"Oh boy, I really hope that I don't screw the pooch on this one . . ."

Having rejected the pleas of the 1st Continental Congress, the British government declared Massachusetts to be in rebellion and ordered troops under General Thomas Gage to seize military supplies from the militia in *Lexington & Concord*, and to arrest patriot leaders Samuel Adams and John Hancock.
Alerted by *Paul Revere* and two other riders, colonial *minute-men* skirmished with the redcoats at Lexington, suffering eight deaths among the casualties.
Having failed to find the patriot leaders,
Gage's troops retreated to Boston, suffering several hundred casualties from colonial forces that harassed them along the way. These *"shots heard 'round the world"* would begin the American War for Independence, with the first actual pitched battle taking place on June 17, 1775 at the *Battle of Bunker Hill*, which actually took place at Breed's Hill.
Although the patriot forces had to retreat when they ran out of ammunition, they would achieve a moral victory having inflicted more than 1,000 casualties upon their better-supplied and more experienced adversaries.

"So how does this sound-
'Dear Georgie, it's not you, it's us...'"
"Too casual? Should I put in something about life & liberty?"
"A lot of us still have slaves, you know ...
This could get kind of awkward;
God, I hate break-ups."

The *2nd Continental Congress* gathered in May, 1775
and created the Continental Army under the command of
George Washington, to be sent into battle against the British
in Massachusetts. Concurrently, the congress sent the
Olive Branch Petition directly to *King George III*
beseeching his intervention on their behalf.
The king rejected this entreaty and instead instituted the
Prohibitory Act which declared all 13 colonies to be
in a state of rebellion and which forbade all commerce
between the colonies and England.
In June of 1776 upon the suggestion of *Richard Henry Lee,*
a committee including *Thomas Jefferson* composed the
Declaration of Independence,
signed by 56 delegates on *July 4th, 1776,*
in which the colonies detailed their expectations
for their government,
the king and Parliament's failure to meet these expectations,
and the consequent severing of all ties with Great Britain.

"Life, liberty &
the pursuit of happiness?"
"I'd give my right arm
for a snow-blower and
some thermal underwear."

The early years of the war went poorly for the Continental troops, with Washington's forces barely escaping capture and losing both New York and Philadelphia to the British. The low point for the patriots was the winter of 1777-1778 which was spent under great duress encamped at *Valley Forge*. Occasional successes such as the Battle of Trenton in 1776 sustained the ill-equipped volunteers, who depended on the unreliable contributions of the various colonial legislatures and the virtually worthless paper money issued by the Continental Congress.

"I know;
let's give those scrappy, upstart Americans our support."

"What harm could possibly come of abetting a popular revolution
against a hereditary monarch?"
"Huzzah, I say!"

The turning-point of the war took place at the
Battle of Saratoga in October of 1777.
Forces under Generals Horatio Gates and Benedict Arnold
defeated three British forces attempting to sever
New England from the other colonies.
As a consequence of the American victory,
King Louis XVI of France decided to openly support
the colonial cause, and it would be thanks to
French financial, military & naval support
that the colonists would ultimately prevail.

"No, there weren't actually camels at the Battle of Yorktown."

"You know what else weren't there? British reinforcements."

The final meaningful battle of the Revolutionary War
would take place at *Yorktown*, Virginia.
A large British army under General *Cornwallis*
sought extraction by sea,
but a French fleet led by Admiral DeGrasse
cut off the Royal Navy and Cornwallis
had to surrender to Washington.
The war would formally end in 1783 with the signing of
the *Treaty of Paris* which stipulated that Great Britain
recognized the independence of the *United States of America*
with a western boundary of the Mississippi River,
that American fishermen could ply the waters off of Canada,
and that debts owed to loyalists and British merchants
would be fulfilled.

"This is so liberating,
living with no centralized
government dictating
what I can & cannot do;
Now if I could just vote
or own property
or go to college or…"

Hesitant to exchange one oppressive centralized authority
for another, the colonies aligned in 1781 according to the
Articles of Confederation.
The Articles created a congress made up of a
single house in which each state had an equal vote.
There was neither an executive nor a judicial branch,
and the congress had no power to tax or compel obedience.
A vote of 9 of the 13 states was required to pass legislation,
and unanimity was required for amendment of the Articles.
One noteworthy accomplishment achieved under the Articles
was the *Land Ordinance of 1785* which established
the procedure for territories to be surveyed and organized into
townships of 36 square miles, with parcels of one square mile
being sold to fund the government,
save a single parcel set aside to fund public education.
The *Northwest Ordinance of 1787*
provided for the division of the Old Northwest Territory
to be divided into the states of Ohio, Indiana, Illinois,
Michigan & Wisconsin, which were all to be admitted on an
equal basis to the original 13 states
and which all forbade slavery.

"We're not paying these taxes and nobody can make us."

"How many militias? Four, you say?"

"Lucky for you I've got crops to harvest so we're going home,
but I'll have you know that I have every intention of
writing a strongly worded letter to my representative."

The weakness of the government created by
the Articles of Confederation became painfully evident in 1786
when Massachusetts farmers led by Revolutionary War
veteran *Daniel Shays* rose up in response to foreclosures on
their properties, high taxes, and debtors' prisons.
Shays and his followers attacked tax collectors and
forced the closure of debtors' courts.
When Shays attacked the arsenal at Springfield,
his rebellion was put down by the militias of four states.
Shays' Rebellion laid bare the potential for
political and social instability under
the Articles of Confederation and alarmed
the more established citizens of the United States,
with *James Madison* and *Alexander Hamilton* calling for the
Annapolis Convention in 1786 to address the deficiencies of
the Articles. When only five states sent delegates, another
convention was called for the next year in Philadelphia at
which all states save Rhode Island would have representatives.

"No; as I've told you again and again,
it is <u>not</u> the opposite of 'prostitution.'"

"'stitution' isn't even a word!"

55 delegates from 12 states would meet over the summer of 1787, ostensibly to revise the Articles but ultimately to write the *Constitution* of the United States.

Meeting in Philadelphia, private deliberations resulted in the creation of a federal system with key powers delegated to the national government and other powers reserved for the states.

Ultimately, a number of key compromises would lead to the Constitution that emerged to be voted upon by the 13 states.

"And where exactly would you suggest I put
a second and a third branch? Idiot!"

Hoping to avoid the concentration of too much power
in any single component of the government, the Constitution
was organized with a *separation of powers* between
legislative, executive and judicial branches.
A system of *"checks & balances"* was implemented under
which the President could *veto* legislation,
Congress could *override* said veto,
the *Senate* had to confirm presidential appointments,
and a *Supreme Court* could rule on disagreements.
The direct voice of the people was muted, with only members
of the *House of Representatives* elected directly
by the adult, white male population.
Senators were to be elected by the various state legislatures,
the president by the *electoral college*,
and judges appointed by the president
with Senate confirmation.

'Well I think that congressional representation
should be based on size!"

Smaller states fearful of being dominated by their more populous neighbors supported the *New Jersey Plan* in which each state would continue to have a single equal vote as existed under the Articles of Confederation.
The *Virginia Plan* proposed a unicameral legislature in which representation would be based upon population.
The *Connecticut* or *Great Compromise* crafted a solution in which a *bicameral legislature* would have a *House of Representatives* based upon the population of each state counterbalanced by a *Senate* in which each state would receive two votes.

"Well how many do I count for?"
"This is ridiculous!"

The *3/5^{ths} Compromise*
resolved the issue of how African-American slaves
would be counted toward representation in Congress.
In exchange for allowing southern states to count each slave as
3/5 of a person for purposes of representation,
the delegates agreed to allow for the banning of the
importation of slaves after 20 years.

"I just can't find it in here anywhere..."

Each of the 13 states had incorporated a *Bill of Rights* into their state constitutions. Several states were hesitant to ratify the Constitution without a Bill of Rights present to restrain the power of the national government. Opponents felt that specifically articulating certain rights might imply the exclusion of others. When Federalists promised to address the absence as a first order of business upon ratification, enough states fell in line to ensure ratification. With New Hampshire voting "yes" in June of 1788 the total of nine states necessary for ratification was reached. With populous Virginia and New York still holding out, however, the union could not be considered secure.

"This is never going to convince anyone; there's no pictures!"
"People are never going to read all this bloviating;
You're definitely looking at this page and completely ignoring
the text on the right, aren't you?"
"Haven't you heard that a picture is worth a thousand words?"
"Get some cartoons in here or we're never going to sniff ratification."

Ratification of the Constitution would occupy the nation from September of 1787 until June of 1788.
Those in favor of ratification became known as *Federalists* and were comprised of the wealthier, more cosmopolitan citizens, while the less affluent and more rural opposition came to be known as *Anti-Federalists*.
In an effort to sway New Yorkers to the Federalist side a series of 85 essays that would come to be known as *The Federalist Papers* were anonymously published by *Alexander Hamilton, James Madison, & John Jay*.
These essays addressed the concerns of voters sufficiently to see New York ratify the Constitution by a narrow margin of 30-27.

"Well, thank goodness that's all worked out;
If we were able to resolve these differences,
I have no doubt that there will ever be political divisions
that our leaders won't be able to resolve.
Thank God we won't have to worry about partisanship from now on!"

Federalist leaders in Virginia including George Washington,
James Madison & John Marshall effectively persuaded enough
of their fellow citizens to ratify the Constitution
in spite of opposition from Anti-Federalist leaders such as
Patrick Henry who feared the establishment of
another authoritarian centralized government.
With New York's subsequent ratification,
hold-outs North Carolina and Rhode Island
eventually acquiesced and the United States of America
was established with the Constitution recognized as
the *"supreme law of the land."*

"As you all know, I cannot tell a lie—
Not only am I the only president elected unanimously
by the electoral college,
but both the nation's capital & a state will be named for me."
"Let's see you top that, John Adams."

George Washington was elected our nation's first president, and chose for his two most influential advisors *Thomas Jefferson* as Secretary of State & *Alexander Hamilton* as Secretary of the Treasury. Hamilton implemented a three-point plan for economic stability that included the chartering of a *national bank*, the implementation of a *tariff* to generate revenue and protect nascent American industries, and the *assumption of all debts* that the Continental Congress had accrued as well as all debts owed by the states. Hamilton hoped to establish the credit-worthiness of the young country and to give its creditors a vested stake in its continued success.

"I hate paying taxes!"

"Me too!"

"We have a lot of whiskey."

"We do indeed."

"Let's get hammered and attack the tax collectors!"

"Sure; what could go wrong?"

"Bottoms up!"

In 1794, farmers in western Pennsylvania
revolted against paying an excise tax on whiskey.
Eager to demonstrate the federal government's strength,
Washington authorized Hamilton to lead a force of
15,000 militiamen against the farmers
who had attacked the tax collectors.
The almost immediate and overwhelming defeat of
the *Whiskey Rebellion* confirmed the authority of the
federal government, but also led to resentment
against the government on the part of backwoods farmers who
would ultimately coalesce into the
Democratic-Republican Party that would soon eclipse
the Federalist Party and which would
elect Thomas Jefferson president in 1800.

""You'd think that with
3,000 miles of ocean
between us & Europe,
we wouldn't have to deal
with this nonsense."
"And as if that weren't sufficiently annoying,
we have to wear these stupid hats!"

The greatest foreign threat faced during the Washington administration was that posed by the war being waged between Great Britain and France. Both sides harassed American shipping, but Washington feared that the United States was still too weak to safely become involved. When Washington issued a *Neutrality Proclamation* in 1793, Jefferson left the cabinet, outraged that the United States was not honoring the Franco-American Treaty entered into during the Revolutionary War.

John Jay would negotiate an unpopular treaty with Great Britain in 1794 which failed to address the issue of the British Navy *impressing* American sailors but in which the British agreed to evacuate forts on the American frontier. Fearing that England and the US were maintaining peaceful relations that might threaten their interests, in 1795 Spain negotiated *Pinkney's Treaty* with the US in which the *right of deposit* was granted to American shippers using the port of *New Orleans* and the *31ˢᵗ Parallel* was recognized as the border between the US and Spanish Florida.

"I may have broken the law by bringing British technology
to America, but big opportunities loomed."

"Get it? Maybe I'll invent stand-up too and take this act on the road."

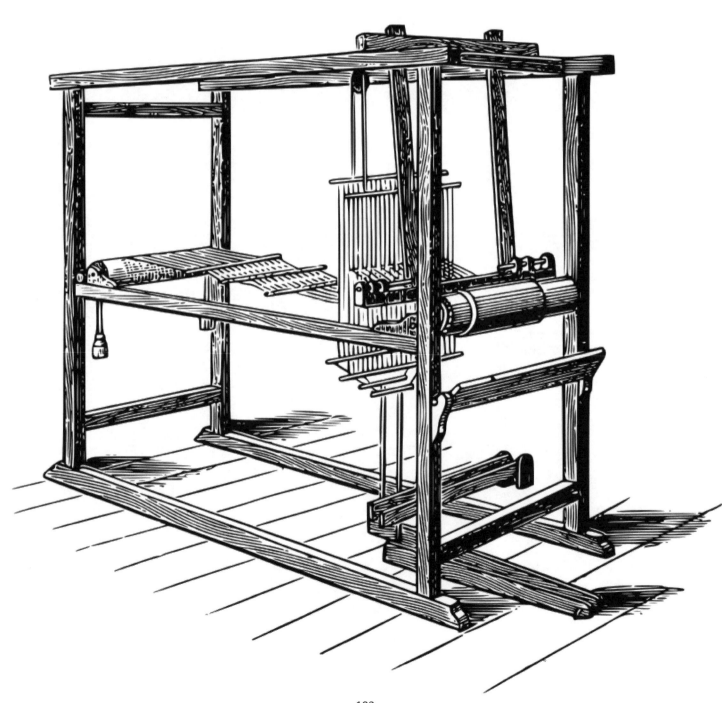

In 1790. factory foreman *Samuel Slater* immigrated from
England to the United States in secret and recreated
from memory spinning, carding & weaving machines
that would make him rich and which would establish the
textile industry as America's
first major manufacturing venture.
Powered by waterwheels and largely centered in
New England, the textile industry would flourish under the
Lowell System pioneered by Cabot Lowell in Massachusetts.
Utilizing primarily young unmarried women for labor,
"company towns" such as Lowell, Massachusetts
became the center of the burgeoning industry which would
grow fifty-fold by the middle of the 1800's.
The textile mills would provide many women with their
first opportunity to find work beyond the family farm.

"Granted, it did help to cause the Civil War,
but without cotton cultivation,
we wouldn't have Q-Tips, so it seems like a reasonable trade-off."
"Remember—you're not supposed to use them in your ears!"

In 1793, while working as a tutor on a southern plantation, New Englander *Eli Whitney* developed an invention which would change the course of history.

Cotton was a luxury item due to the labor-intensive nature of removing the seeds from the fiber. Whitney's invention of the *Cotton Gin* would enable a single worker operating the machine to process 50 pounds of cotton a day, as opposed to one pound which could be cleaned by hand.

This invention made the cultivation of cotton in the south incredibly lucrative for plantation owners and made practical the continued utilization of slave labor, which would likely otherwise have diminished.

While cotton cultivation was exclusively a southern pursuit in the United States, northern textile mills, banks and shippers all profited off of what became the most valuable commodity in the United States.

Interestingly, Whitney would go on to perfect the mass production of rifles thanks to his innovations in machine tools and *interchangeable parts*, so it is in large part due to his influence that the US had cause to fight the Civil War and for the war to be so deadly.

Following his second term, George Washington would opt not to run for re-election, establishing a precedent of no president serving more than two terms that would hold until Franklin Delano Roosevelt won both third and fourth elections. In his *Farewell Address*, Washington also notably *warned against entangling alliances* with foreign powers and *increasing political partisanship*.

John Adams would serve as both the first and the last *Federalist* president, with few noteworthy accomplishments during his administration. Adams would gain respect for standing up to French intimidation during the *XYZ Affair* in which he refused to pay a bribe in order to meet with the French foreign minister.

In an effort to hinder his political opposition, Adams supported the Alien, Sedition & Naturalization Acts. The *Alien Act* allowed for the deportation of perceived foreign threats, the *Sedition Act* made criticism of the government illegal and the *Naturalization Act* nearly tripled the residency requirement for citizenship from 5 to 14 years. In response to these laws, Vice President Thomas Jefferson and James Madison anonymously wrote the *Kentucky & Virginia Resolutions* which stipulated that the states could *nullify* federal laws with which they disagreed, setting a precedent which would ultimately be resolved by the American Civil War.

"We are all Republicans, we are all Federalists."

"But some of us are winners, and some of us are losers,
so know your place."

"No hemming and hawing for me; just Hemings.
That's a history joke; look it up."

In the presidential election of 1800, Democratic-Republican Thomas Jefferson would tie Aaron Burr in the electoral college. With arch-rival Alexander Hamilton throwing New York's support in the House of Representatives behind him, Jefferson would be elected and establish the precedent of the peaceful transition of power from the administration of one political party to another.

Jefferson's *Democratic-Republican* Party was one that espoused smaller government and championed the yeoman farmer versus the wealthy elites, and found its support in the south and west as opposed to New England which remained the province of the Federalists.

Jefferson's *strict constructionist* attitude stipulated that the federal government was limited in its power and scope to that which was specifically and literally articulated in the Constitution, as opposed to the *loose constructionist* approach that maintained that the federal government could do anything that was not specifically prohibited. This attitude would be tested by Jefferson's greatest accomplishment as president, the acquisition for the United States of the *Louisiana Purchase.*

It's a good thing they had Sacagawea for a guide;
two men would have never stopped to ask for directions;
they might still be out there now!

Concerned that American farmers in the west would lose access to the port of New Orleans given that Spain had ceded control of Louisiana to France, Jefferson authorized an offer of $10,000,000 for New Orleans and a strip of land eastward toward Florida. Anxious about having to defend Louisiana against the British and no longer needing it to supply Haiti following its successful slave revolt led by Toussaint Louverture, Napoleon offered all of Louisiana to the United States for *$15,000,000*.
Although conflicted, Jefferson made the purchase and more than doubled the size of the United States, which would now stretch from the Atlantic Ocean to the Rocky Mountains.
In 1804, Jefferson would authorize a surveying trip under *Lewis & Clark* guided in part by *Sacagawea* which would spend two years traversing the west, helping to establish American claims to the *Oregon Territory*.

Pioneers such as Boone might have faced less of a challenge had they mastered the art of marksmanship.

Pioneers such as *Daniel Boone* eagerly headed west and settled
America's new frontier.
Boone, a veteran of both the French & Indian and
Revolutionary Wars, had much earlier traversed
the *Cumberland Gap* and settled in Kentucky,
where he would be followed by thousands of others eager to
establish farms and homesteads of their own.
Boone would end up being captured by Native Americans,
escaping and relocating even farther west to Missouri.
The adventurous spirit of Americans such as Boone helped
to populate the west, but also led to conflict with
and destruction of native populations,
and also the spread of slavery far beyond its original boundaries.

"Is this what everyone means by
'Marshall law?'"

"Actually, it's not."

1803 saw a final triumph for the Federalist Party and for the Supreme Court as a co-equal branch of the national government. Chief Justice *John Marshall* ruled in *Marbury v. Madison* that 16 "midnight" judicial appointments made by John Adams as his term expired would not take effect. Marshall's ruling was a short-term victory for his cousin and political rival President Thomas Jefferson in the sense that the Federalist appointees would not receive their lifetime appointments, but in accepting Marshall's ruling that the Judiciary Act of 1789 by which the appointments had been made had been unconstitutional, the nation acknowledged the right of the federal judiciary to rule on the legitimacy of laws passed by Congress. This power of *judicial review* would time and again play an overwhelmingly important role in the course of United States history.

"Hopefully this ridiculously large wheel will distract anyone from making fun of my ludicrous outfit & mustache."

In 1807, American *Robert Fulton* demonstrated the first successful *steamboat* which harnessed an engine that utilized pressurized steam to turn paddlewheels that propelled the vessel even against river currents. Fulton's *Clermont* made the 300-mile round trip from New York City to Albany and back in 62 hours. The ability of Fulton's ship to transport people and goods speedily and regardless of current revolutionized shipping and commerce and helped to open the interior of the United States to development.

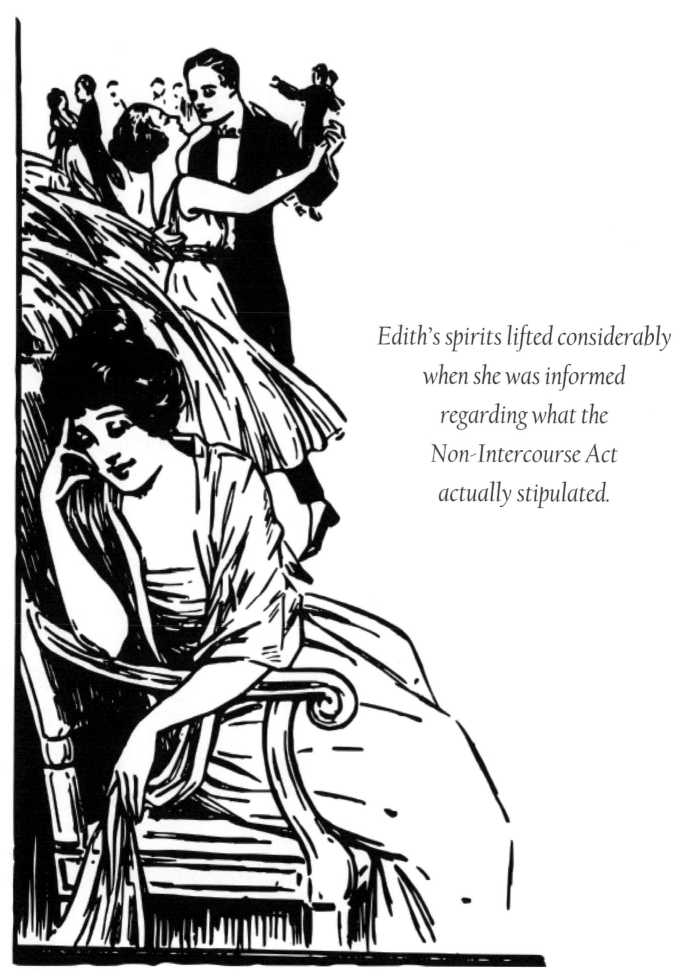

Edith's spirits lifted considerably when she was informed regarding what the Non-Intercourse Act actually stipulated.

All was not so positive for President Jefferson
in the realm of foreign affairs.
As war continued to rage between Napoleon and his enemies,
both France and Great Britain posed a threat to
American shipping. Having initially forbidden all American
ships from traveling to foreign ports with the *Embargo Act* of
1807, Jefferson relented shortly thereafter as his policy's
greatest impact had been upon American commerce and not
foreign aggressors. Newly-elected President *James Madison*
followed with the *Non-Intercourse Act* of 1809 which
allowed trade with all nations save France & Great Britain.
Macon's Bill #2 stipulated that the US would resume trade
with whichever nation first pledged to respect
American neutrality. France did so, although continued to
seize American merchant ships regardless, and the escalating
naval tension with Great Britain helped to bring about what
many consider the second war of American independence,
the *War of 1812.*

"Well, we may not have beaten the British this time,
but a tie is still nothing to sneeze at, right?"

"I mean, Napoleon couldn't defeat them either,
so we're not losers or anything."

"If we had actually been defeated, we'd all be speaking English today…"

Continued harassment of American shipping by the Royal Navy combined with a lust for battle on the part of young Republicans in Congress such as *Henry Clay & John C. Calhoun* who became known as *"War Hawks"* led Madison to ask for a declaration of war in June of 1812. By this time the British had agreed to cease naval hostilities, but word reached Washington too late.

The war would ultimately be fought to a tie, with an ill-advised American invasion of Canada and the burning of Washington DC in 1814. American naval forces would fare better in the *Battle of Lake Erie* and the *Battle of Lake Champlain*.

Ironically, the greatest American victory of the war at the *Battle of New Orleans* in 1815 would also take place after the signing of the *Treaty of Ghent* ended the war in 1815, but once again the news took too long to reach the combatants to avoid several thousand lives lost.

*While the moonwalk
is undoubtedly impressive,
Michael was likely
not the Jackson whose moves would
have the greatest impact
upon US history.*

Gaining national prominence in the War of 1812,
General *Andrew Jackson* would go on to have a tremendous
impact upon the nation.
A self-made backwoodsman who became a wealthy
plantation-owner in Tennessee.
Jackson's toughness and resolve would make him a hero
to the American "common man" and would propel him
to election to both the House of Representatives and the Senate
and eventually to two terms as President.

"Give me a break;
California and Texas aren't even part of the union yet!"

"Why don't you just throw Alaska & Hawaii on here too,
and give me even more to have to juggle?"

Another western politician who would have a powerful
and enduring impact upon US history was
Henry Clay of Kentucky. Ultimately rising to Speaker of the
House, Secretary of State, and a candidate for president on
multiple occasions, Clay proposed what became known as the
"American System."
Clay's three-point plan called for a re-chartering
of the *national bank*, the implementation of a substantial *tariff*
to protect the young American manufacturers who had
organized during the interruption of commerce during the
preceding hostilities with Great Britain, and support for
internal improvements that would link the country together
such as roads, bridges and canals.
Ever the politician who would seek compromise,
the wily Clay sought something for New England, the south
and the west. His efforts to balance benefits for all sections of
the country would be met with occasional resistance, but Clay
succeeded in laying a foundation that would bring growth
to all regions of the expanding nation.

"Is there any chance we could be paid by the blister rather than by the hour?"
"My manicure is going to be ruined."

With strict constructionist *James Monroe's* election as president in 1816, federal support for intrastate development was non-existent. Governor *De Witt Clinton* of New York would embark on the most expensive construction project in the young nation's history with the excavation of the *Erie Canal* from 1817-1825.

34 locks would accommodate a nearly 600 foot elevation change on the 363 mile canal and allow flatboats to connect the Great Lakes at Buffalo to the Hudson River at Albany, opening the interior of the US up to Atlantic shipping. The project cost just over $7,100,000 ($116,000,000 in 2020) and lowered shipping costs by 95%.

What many had deemed "*Clinton's Folly*" quickly transformed the economy of the region and soon turned a profit as well.

"Well, this would have certainly made things a heck of a lot easier; why didn't one of you genius inventors get ahead of the curve on this one?"

Although canals could move people and goods
more cheaply and more quickly, northern canals became
useless in winter and needed a nearby source of water to keep
them filled. Roads became an important part of economic
growth, with some toll roads funded privately and other roads
funded by states and, occasionally, the national government.
The *Lancaster Turnpike* connected
Philadelphia and Lancaster Pennsylvania
with a reliable cobblestone road in the 1790's,
but the most significant early road was the
Cumberland (National) Road built between 1811 & 1838
that ultimately linked the Potomac River at
Cumberland, Maryland with the Ohio River at
Wheeling, (West) Virginia and eventually
Vandalia, Illinois 620 miles to the west.

"That stuffy old John Adams never made me feel this way;
the Democratic-Republicans are definitely the people's party,
that's for sure. The pursuit of happiness rules."

With the exception of John Marshall's 34-year stranglehold on control of the Supreme Court,
after the fiasco of the *Hartford Convention* in which Federalist New Englanders schemed to break away from the US near the end of the War of 1812, the Federalist Party effectively ceased to exist on the national level.
The Monroe administration would preside over a period of single-party rule from 1816-1824 that has come to be known as *"The Era of Good Feelings."*
While sectional squabbles and rural/urban distinctions continued to exist, policy was largely the province of the *Democratic-Republicans*.
Monroe's second election would see him run essentially unopposed, with but a single electoral vote being denied him merely to ensure that George Washington would remain the only president ever elected unanimously by the electoral college.

And where would we be without America's kickstand?
We definitely needed somewhere for shirtless inbreeds to wrestle gators
and prove Darwin was right.

In pursuit of Seminole raiding parties operating out of Spanish Florida, Andrew Jackson led a militia across the border into Spanish territory, killing several Seminole chiefs and two British traders, in addition to burning the Seminole villages. This would ultimately lead to the *Adams-Onis Treaty* of 1819 in which Spain ceded *Florida* to the United States in exchange for the US assuming $5,000,000 in claims against the Spanish and a guarantee that the US would respect Spanish control of *Texas.*

"Just so we're all in agreement,
we're fine with slavery as long as it's not
in our backyard."
"It's not like this is the first time
basic human rights have been denied
for political expediency;
I mean, you've read the preceding pages, right?"

Sectional differences nearly came to a head in 1820 with
Missouri's application for entry into the union as a slave state.
Fearing that a precedent would be set allowing slavery
in the states created from the land acquired via the
Louisiana Purchase and fearful of upsetting the balance of
11 free states and 11 slave states, *Henry Clay* suggested a
solution that became known as the *Missouri Compromise*.
Missouri was to be admitted as a slave state,
Maine was to be made a free state separate from
Massachusetts, and slavery would be thenceforth prohibited
from new states above Missouri's southern border at *36° 30'*.
This compromise would endure until 1850,
but the issue of slavery would continue to fester until
it would finally be resolved by the Civil War.

"And all I'm saying is don't cross this line and there won't be any problems...."

Shortly before leaving the White House,
President Monroe in 1823 articulated what would come to be
a cornerstone of US foreign policy over the next 200 years
when he issued the *Monroe Doctrine*.
Following an initial suggestion from the British that
the two nations should jointly warn other European powers
against expansion or colonization in the Americas,
Secretary of State *John Quincy Adams* instead persuaded
President Monroe to issue a unilateral declaration that
the US would not tolerate foreign intrusions
on our side of the Atlantic.
Although likely too weak to enforce the doctrine initially,
Adams counted on the threat of British naval strength
discouraging any subsequent European adventurism.
The Monroe Doctrine would not be significantly tested
for many years, but over time the US would be largely
successful in forestalling foreign meddling in the Americas.

"Even I can see that there's something shady going on around here."

The election of 1824 brought the Era of Good Feelings to a
close when four candidates split the electoral vote, again
throwing the decision into the House of Representatives.
As the lowest vote-getter, Speaker of the House Henry Clay
was eliminated, and William Crawford suffered a stroke
leaving *Andrew Jackson & John Quincy Adams*
to vie for the White House.
In what came to be regarded as the *"Corrupt Bargain,"*
Clay threw his support behind Adams
in exchange for Adams naming Clay Secretary of State.
Jackson, who had earned the plurality of both
the popular and electoral votes was outraged
and would run successfully in 1828 and 1832,
fissuring the Democratic-Republican party
and beginning the era of *Jacksonian Democracy*.

"*Let me just explain to you how this is going to go down . . .*"

In spite of being an avowed champion of the "little guy"
and a life-long advocate of *states' rights*,
Andrew Jackson would find himself staunchly defending
the authority of the federal government in what would become
known as the *nullification crisis*.
In response to the increased rates passed in the 1828
"Tariff of Abominations," South Carolina, covertly led by
Vice President *John C. Calhoun*, voted to *nullify* the tariff.
Even when a reduced rate was introduced in the Tariff of 1832,
South Carolina continued its recalcitrance.
Jackson persuaded Congress to pass the *Force Bill*
which authorized military action against South Carolina
for its refusal to allow collection of the tariff.
Although Jackson's strong response avoided an armed conflict
for the time being, the issue of
state sovereignty vs. the federal government
would not ultimately be resolved until the Civil War.

"You're right; it has been a minute since they broke a treaty with us."
"It's a good thing we've got John Marshall and the Supreme Court
on our side, or we'd be really screwed."

Jackson's regard for the people
did not extend to all the people.
Not only was Jackson a substantial slaveholder,
but in 1830 Jackson signed the *Indian Removal Act*
which allowed Georgia to steal the land of the *Cherokee* tribe
in exchange for the promise of land in the west that would
ultimately be taken again and turned into the
state of *Oklahoma*. The Supreme Court ruled in
Worcester v. Georgia that Georgia had no authority within
the Cherokee nation, to which Jackson apocryphally replied
"John Marshall has made his ruling, now let him enforce it."
Despite the Court's decision, in 1838 the US forced
over 15,000 Cherokee to trek from Georgia to Oklahoma,
a wintertime journey of despair that cost over a quarter of the
Cherokee their lives, and all of them their homes.

*"If you want my two cents,
the bank should have been protected."*

*"And, bacon clogs your arteries,
so maybe have oatmeal for breakfast, instead."*

Jackson's final successful power-play would involve
the *2nd Bank of the United States*.
Jackson believed that the bank favored the wealthy elites
and opposed its concentration of influence upon the economy.
Jackson's rival *Henry Clay* orchestrated an early vote
to re-charter the bank in 1832, thinking that Jackson's hostility
to the bank could be utilized as ammunition
against Jackson in the election. Clay miscalculated,
and Jackson won re-election with more than
75% of the electoral vote.
Jackson took this as a mandate to destroy the bank,
and during his second term Jackson withdrew all federal funds
from the bank, instead distributing them to various
state-chartered banks. These poorly-regulated and unreliable
banks would prove to be dysfunctional,
and shortly after Jackson's second term
the economy crashed in the *Panic of 1837*.

"Now that you mention it,
I think that a wig would have to be
a major improvement."

"Oh, umm . . . that's awkward;
never mind."

Andrew Jackson was one of our most polarizing presidents, and his impact led to a resumption of two-party politics. The *Whigs* emerged as an alternative to the Democratic Party, but their influence would be short-lived and would ultimately elect only two presidents, both war heroes who would die prior to the end of their terms.

William Henry Harrison, made famous at the *Battle of Tippecanoe* in 1811 during which he led an Indiana militia of 1,000 men and defeated a Native American confederation of tribes led by *Tecumseh & Tenskwatawa*, gave history's longest inaugural address outside in the rain, caught pneumonia and died within a month, becoming the first president to die in office. *John Tyler*, an avowed Democrat whose personal antipathy for Jackson led him to join the Whig ticket as vice president, became the first vice president to assume the presidency due to his running-mate's death. The Whigs would elect Mexican War hero *Zachary Taylor* in 1848, who would also die in office and be followed by an equally unremarkable vice president in Millard Fillmore.

.-..-. - .... . .-. . .--- ... / -. --- / .-- .- - -.-- / -.-- ---

..- / --. .-- / - --- / - .... . / - -. --- ..- -.-. -.. . / ---

..-. / - -. .- - ... -... . - .. -. --. / - .... -.-. / ..

..-. / -.-- --- ..- / -.. --- --.-- / -.-- --- ..- / -. . .-.. /

- --- / --. . .- / .- / .-... ....- . .-.- -.-.

"You probably don't know Morse Code,
but trust me-if you did, this would be hilarious."

Seldom have inventions had as rapid and significant an impact
upon a nation and its people as did the *railroad* and
the *telegraph*. Introduced to the United States in 1828,
the steam-powered locomotive would allow for the
rapid population and exploitation of the United States
as it expanded across the continent.
The railroads would quickly become
the nation's leading industry, which would itself drive the
growth of other ventures such as steel-making and ranching.
The federal government would make grants of millions of acres
of land to railroads for rights-of-way and
to sell in order to fund their capital-intensive construction.
Frequently running alongside the tracks beginning in 1844
were telegraph wires which enabled near-instantaneous
communication over the vast nation.
Created by *Samuel F.B. Morse*, the telegraph hastened
the nation's development at the speed of electricity.

"The plow is great,
but I'm still spending 12 hours a day
on the south side of a northbound horse. This job stinks."

The Great Plains, now easily accessible and available
for large-scale planting and ranching became viable
thanks to the invention in 1837 of the self-scouring *steel plow*.
Developed by *John Deere*,
the *"plow that broke the plains"*
replaced iron and wood plows that couldn't break through the
fertile but compacted soil that had been trod upon
by millions of bison, elk, and antelope for centuries.

"No, thankfully it was not
that kind of reaper."
"That having been said,
I'm killing it out here."

Cyrus McCormick would perfect a *mechanical reaper* pulled by horses that would be able to effectively harvest the bountiful crops planted on the Great Plains. Beginning in 1845, farmers using McCormick's reaper could perform the work that would have previously taken five men working with scythes

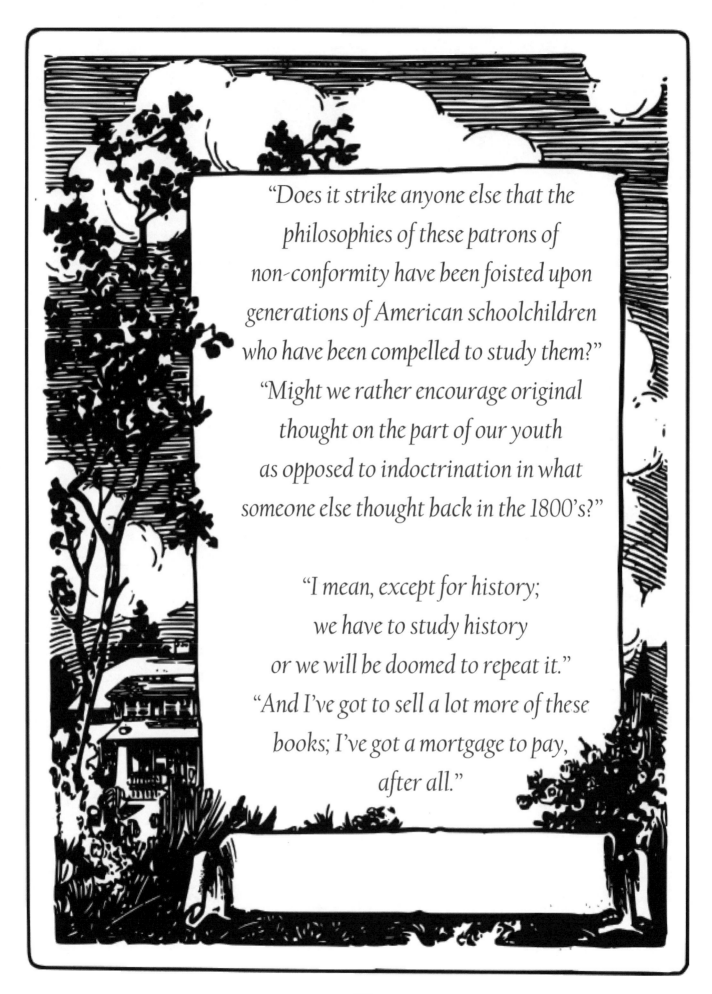

"Does it strike anyone else that the
philosophies of these patrons of
non-conformity have been foisted upon
generations of American schoolchildren
who have been compelled to study them?"
"Might we rather encourage original
thought on the part of our youth
as opposed to indoctrination in what
someone else thought back in the 1800's?"

"I mean, except for history;
we have to study history
or we will be doomed to repeat it."
"And I've got to sell a lot more of these
books; I've got a mortgage to pay,
after all."

Changes in the United States during the *antebellum period*
went beyond technological innovation, land acquisition,
and political and economic evolution.
Transcendentalism, a distinctly American school of philosophy
embraced nature and the value of self-expression as opposed to
more traditional religious, philosophical and political doctrines.
Ralph Waldo Emerson championed *self-reliance* and
admonished *"to thine own self, be true."*
Henry David Thoreau lived apart from society in a small cabin
by Walden Pond, where he cultivated his theory of
civil disobedience which would manifest itself first
in his being jailed for having refused to pay taxes that supported
the American war in Mexico
and which would later be adopted by civil rights icons such as
Mahatma Gandhi and Dr. Martin Luther King, Jr.

"Celibacy? Seriously?"

"And you honestly expect this movement to be successful?"

Several communities would embrace non-traditional lifestyles during the mid-19th century.
Among the most prominent
of these *utopian communities* were:
the *Shakers*, noted for their abstinence from sex;
New Harmony, Indiana which followed
a proto-socialist lifestyle;
Oneida, New York which was dedicated to
equality, communal living and free love; &
Brook Farm, Massachusetts where Emerson himself lived with
others according to Transcendentalist principles.

"You think you've got problems?"

"I've got four different wives telling me I don't know where I'm going."

Countering the more progressive philosophies of
the utopian communities were the resurgent Calvinist
principles of the *2nd Great Awakening*.
Beginning in 1823 in what came to be known as the
"burned-over district" of upstate New York thanks to the
"fire & brimstone" sermons of *evangelists* such as
Charles Grandison Finney, *Baptists* and *Methodists* spread
the word of faith in God and the need for Christians to be
"born again" in order to achieve salvation.
Concurrently, a distinctly American faith emerged when
Joseph Smith unveiled the *Book of Mormon* that he claimed
had been revealed to him by the angel Moroni,
which detailed how Jesus had visited North America before its
discovery by Europeans and which shared God's final
instructions for mankind. Among the beliefs of the
Church of Jesus Christ of Latter-Day Saints was that a man
should take multiple wives in order to be fruitful and multiply.
This adherence to *polygamy* brought harassment from local
communities and drove the Mormons from
New York to Ohio to Illinois where Smith was murdered.
Brigham Young led the remaining members of the church
along the *Mormon Trail*, ultimately settling near
the *Great Salt Lake* in what would become *Utah*.

"The Shakers took away sex two pages ago;
now you want us to give up booze? Give me a break, already."

Several powerful social movements gained traction during the middle of the 1800's. Although the abolitionist movement would supersede all others, the *temperance* movement would strive to limit or eliminate the scourge of alcohol from American society.

Maine would become the first state to restrict alcohol manufacturing and sales in 1851 under *Neal Dow*. Over succeeding decades, "dries" ranging from *Carrie Nation* to the *Anti-Saloon League* to the *Women's Christian Temperance Union* would all chip away at the availability of alcohol until *Prohibition* at the national level would be attempted with the ratification of the *18th Amendment* and implementation of the *Volstead Act*.

"You'd have to be crazy
to want to be in a place like this."

Dorothea Dix made noteworthy contributions to the humane treatment of both criminals and the mentally ill. Whereas earlier American punishment had been chiefly limited to corporal punishment or capital punishment, the *penitentiary* system was established to give criminals a chance to reflect upon their actions and subsequently reform.

The mentally ill had at best been warehoused to protect society from the threat they were perceived to pose, but Dix led a movement for treatment in less-restrictive sanitariums in which they could be treated by the new field of psychology. A chance to be heard and productive led to genuine strides in the well-being of these less-fortunate Americans.

"Screw you, Horace Mann."

Educational reform would help to make the United States one of the most literate and broadly-educated nations in the world. The concept of public funds being spent on public education which went back to the *Land Ordinance of 1785* would lead to nearly-universal public grammar schools, with the notable and unfair exception of African-American & Native American youth. Following the lead of Massachusetts Secretary of Education *Horace Mann*, communities around the country funded instruction for boys and girls, at least through the 8th grade. *"Normal schools"* were also fostered to cultivate a generation of competent teachers for America's youth. Colleges such as *Mount Holyoke* in Massachusetts and *Oberlin College* in Ohio would be among the first to provide higher educational opportunities for women, and a handful of colleges including Oberlin would even admit non-white students as well.

"Cult of Domesticity, my rear;
If women could vote, I wouldn't have to be out here
busting my hump taking care of these jerks."

As the United States began to transition from
an overwhelmingly agrarian society to one in which
many families made their living through
manufacturing, commerce or trades,
family size shrank from an average of over seven members
prior to the Revolutionary War to
approximately five by a century later.
With more men working six days a week,
up to 12 hours a day outside the home,
it was expected that a wife,
in addition to all of her other household duties
would serve as a teacher and moral exemplar for her family.
This *"cult of domesticity"* lionized traditional feminine
gender roles, but made the battle for feminine equality
that much more arduous.

*"I realize change isn't going to
happen overnight,
but would it be too much to ask for
a pair of shoes, at least?"
"Stupid patriarchy."*

As leading proponents of many social reform movements,
it was only natural that women would address
their own status as second-class citizens
within the United States of America.
Pioneering feminists such as
Lucretia Mott, *Elizabeth Cady Stanton* & *Susan B. Anthony*
would advocate for educational opportunities,
employment options, property rights & most importantly
political equality in the form of voting rights.
These *suffragettes* would gather at *Seneca Falls*, New York
in 1848 to issue a *"Declaration of Sentiments"*
in which they detailed their plight and
articulated their demands for gender equality.
The women's movement would take a back seat
to the cause of abolition for many years,
but eventually the right for women to vote would be
guaranteed nation-wide by the ratification
of the *19th Amendment*.

Interesting that half the states that fought for independence from Great Britain were perfectly comfortable keeping a substantial percentage of their population enslaved.

Apparently hypocrisy wasn't a thing in the antebellum south.

Despite the awful repression endured by slaves in America, there were approximately 250 attempted uprisings. Among the most significant were the *Stono Uprising* of 1739, in which approximately 20 slaves killed their captors and escaped retribution for a week while attempting to reach freedom in Spanish Florida. *Denmark Vesey*, a former slave who had purchased his freedom with lottery winnings, attempted to lead a revolt in South Carolina in 1822 but was betrayed by slaves who feared the possible consequences, resulting in Vesey's capture and the execution of 35 African-Americans. In 1831, *Nat Turner* led 70 slaves in Virginia in an insurrection inspired by an eclipse blotting out the sun, metaphorically showing black dominating white. More than 60 whites were killed and Turner escaped capture for six weeks, but was ultimately found and executed along with several hundred other African-Americans, both free and enslaved. After each attempted rebellion, further restrictions were put upon African-Americans in an effort to maintain white domination.

"When will a man's worth be judged by the quality of his character and not the color of his skin?"
(spoiler alert: it's going to be a while.)

One of the most influential voices for political emancipation
of the slaves was *Frederick Douglass*,
himself a former slave who had escaped to freedom in the North.
Douglass would serve as a shining example of the
intellectual potential being suppressed by prejudice,
writing three best-selling memoirs and speaking
passionately and persuasively about the injustice of slavery.
Douglass' irreproachable character, eloquent oratory and
life experience made him an incredibly powerful champion
in the abolitionist movement.
Asserting that he would
"unite with anybody to do right and with nobody to do wrong"
Douglass was a tireless example of the power of an individual
to triumph as a force for good in the world
against the most daunting obstacles.

"I get it; slavery is an atrocity."

"But after 34 years,

would it kill you to include a %#@! sports section?"

Using the platform of the <u>New York Liberator</u>,
publisher *William Lloyd Garrison* attacked the evils of slavery
with passion and without restraint.
An ardent Christian who believed the very Constitution
of the United States was illegitimate
given its tolerance of human bondage,
Garrison would also head the *American Anti-Slavery Society*
and become a champion for women's suffrage.
It was Garrison's newspaper, however, that had the
greatest impact. From its founding in 1831 until emancipation
following the Civil War, Garrison relentlessly attacked the
"peculiar institution." Publishing a *"black list"* of that week's
whippings, executions and slave sales, Garrison was vilified
in the South with a $5,000 bounty put on his head and
the banning of <u>The Liberator</u> throughout the South.
Having attested that
"I am in earnest—I will not equivocate—I will not excuse—
I will not retreat a single inch—and I will be heard,"
Garrison truly demonstrated the power of the press
championed in the 1st Amendment.

"No, it wasn't actually,
and it didn't go underground either."

While 4,000,000 African-Americans would still be enslaved
by the time of the Civil War,
tens of thousands escaped via the *Underground Railroad.*
Relying on a series of safe houses that most often
led north to freedom,
but also south to the Caribbean or Mexico,
"conductors" would lead escaped slaves under cover of night
from 10-20 miles each day.
The dangerous journey would become even more arduous after
the *Fugitive Slave Law* was enacted as part of the
Compromise of 1850. The law would compel free states
to participate in the pursuit and capture of the escaped
"property" of southern slaveholders, although there was often
popular resistance to this in spite of the law.
Harriet Tubman, herself an escaped slave,
would lead 70 slaves to freedom
over 13 missions back down south,
putting her own life and liberty at risk with each trip.

"I'm glad that this is in black & white
so that everyone thinks I struck it rich
when I'm really just posing dramatically with a rock."

Settlement of the west would be accelerated periodically by discoveries of precious gold & silver deposits. A *gold rush* spiked by *Jacob Sutter's* discovery near San Francisco led to a boom of prospectors, prostitutes & entrepreneurs eager to seek their fortunes. *Pike's Peak*, *Colorado* and *Carson City, Nevada* would be among early boomtowns that spurred rapid settlement, and eventually the *Dakota Territory* and even *Alaska* would thrive and suffer due to the avarice of men seeking their fortunes. Although some did indeed achieve great wealth, most individual miners met with frustration, while the greatest wealth was amassed by corporate interests that had the resources to wrest their fortunes from the landscape, often doing significant environmental damage in the process.

"If we can just get this to stretch from the Atlantic to the Pacific, we'll be all good…"

An outlet for American expansion and opportunism
was the driving impetus behind the concept of
Manifest Destiny.
Embracing a spirit of *American exceptionalism* that
maintained that it was God's clear intention for
the United States to stretch
"from sea to shining sea,"
proponents of Manifest Destiny would advocate
for the US to settle the disputed *Oregon Territory*,
dividing control with the British at the *49th parallel*;
would drive the US to annex *Texas* in 1845;
would push the US into the *Mexican War* which would
ultimately lead to the *Mexican Cession*,
an area larger than the Louisiana Purchase;
and would finally culminate with the *Gadsden Purchase*,
intended to facilitate the construction of
the *Southern Pacific Railroad*.

"Is it by any chance called the 'Lone Star State'
because none of the other states want anything to do with it?"
"Just thinking out loud…"

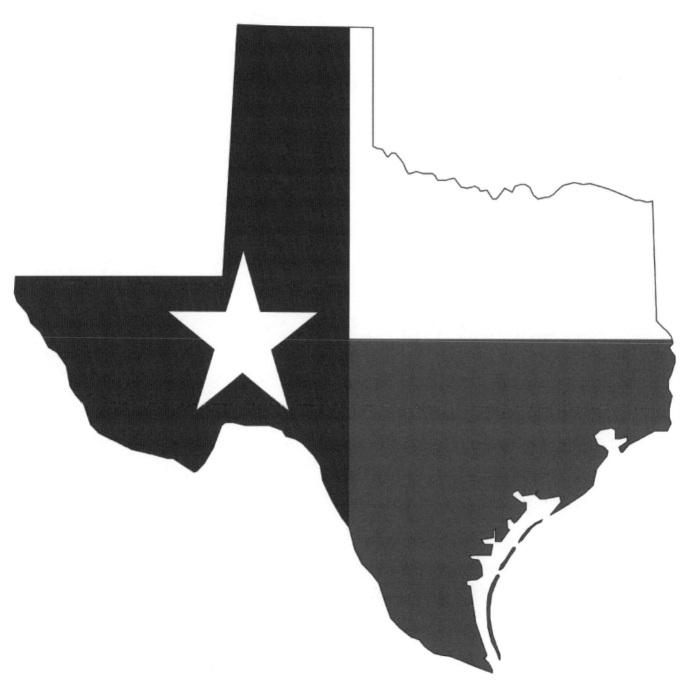

After having won its independence from Spain in 1821,
Mexico, hoping to prevent Comanche incursions by
populating the sparsely-settled region, reached a deal with
Moses Austin to settle 300 American families in *Texas*,
with the understanding that they would convert to
Catholicism and repudiate slavery.
The American would indeed settle in Texas, but would
fail to reject slave ownership.
Tensions would build until eventually,
Texas would battle for its independence from Mexico,
eventually gaining its freedom after battles including
the Alamo and *San Jacinto*.
Davy Crockett, Sam Houston, Jim Bowie & Steven Austin
would be among Texas' founding fathers,
and although Texas immediately petitioned for annexation to
the United States in 1836, hesitancy to admit such a large
territory that would doubtless become slave-holding states
led to resistance in Congress, and Texas would spend
nearly 10 years as an independent nation.

"I'm not saying we _have_ to fight over this,
I'm just saying this gun is loaded."

When the Democratic Party deadlocked on nominating former President Martin Van Buren or Senator John C. Calhoun to run against Henry Clay in 1844, *"dark horse"* candidate *James K. Polk* ended up running and won, becoming America's most successful, least well-known president.

Polk, as promised, served a single term and accomplished every goal to which he had aspired.

The US resolved the *Oregon* dispute with Great Britain;

The US won the *Mexican War* and increased the nation's size by more than 1/3 with the acquisition of the *Mexican Cession* for $18,250,000;

The *Walker Tariff* substantially reduced taxes on imports; & The US reestablished an *independent treasury.*

Polk's term would be followed by the election of Zachary Taylor who would headline a string of inconsequential presidents who would all prove incapable of successfully resolving the nation's biggest domestic challenge, the existence of slavery.

"If this is what you call a compromise,
I say it's about time for us to disagree."

Zachary Taylor would die prior to the end of his term, and his successor Millard Fillmore would ensure the passage of the *Compromise of 1850*, contrived by Senators *Henry Clay & Stephen Douglas*.
The compromise:
Admitted California as a free state;
Created the territories of *Utah & New Mexico* with their slavery status to be determined by *popular sovereignty*,
Compensated Texas with $10,000,000 for land lost to the New Mexico territory;
Banned the slave trade in Washington DC
while still allowing slavery in the nation's capital; &
Enacted a new *Fugitive Slave Law* with compulsory enforcement even in the free states of the North.
While the compromise forestalled division between the slave and free states, it enflamed outrage on both sides, particularly the North in which abolitionists decried having to be party to slave-catching.

"Thanks a lot;
you just blabbed the ending
on the opposite page."
"Now there's not even any point
in finishing this."
"What are you going to tell me next—
that Darth Vader is Luke's father?"

"Jerk!"

Few books have had as great of an impact upon US history as _Uncle Tom's Cabin_. *Harriet Beecher Stowe* came from a family of ardent abolitionists, and when she learned of the outrages inherent in the Compromise of 1850, she wrote what would become one of the most beloved and at the same time most reviled novels in the nation's history.
Telling the story of mistreatment, nobility, suffering & death of kindly Uncle Tom, the beloved protagonist who dies as a result of the cruelty of his overseer Simon LeGree, Uncle Tom's Cabin galvanized support for the abolitionist cause in the North and around the world while stiffening southern resistance to what was considered hateful propaganda written by a northern idealist who had never witnessed the *"peculiar institution"* first-hand.
Banned in the South but read widely everywhere else, the power of the novel was epitomized when *Abraham Lincoln*, upon meeting Stowe, is said to have remarked
"so this is the little woman who caused this great war."

"I don't care what new-fangled party you're referencing,
I'm telling you, there's no such thing as a free lunch!"

"Didn't you have to take Economics in that fancy-pants school
I now have to pay taxes to support?"

Formed as a consequence of the election of 1848
in which neither the Democratic nor the Whig Party
adequately addressed the expansion of slavery to their liking,
the *Free Soil Party* formed and nominated Martin Van Buren
as their candidate, garnering over 10% of the popular vote, the
strongest third-party performance in US history up to that time.
The platform of the new party was simply:

Free Soil;

Free Labor;

Free Speech;

Free Men.

As regional tensions would boil over, the Free Soil Party
would be replaced prior to the election of 1856
by the newly-formed ***Republican Party,***
but the platform for which the party had been created
would eventually be realized in its entirety.

"Hey; not only does this hat work for the Know-Nothing Party, but in a few years I'll be able to repurpose it when I join the Klan once it's invented."

Arising as a consequence of surging *nativism*
in the 1840's & 1850's,
the *American/Know-Nothing Party*
filled a gap between the fading Whig Party
and the as-yet unformed Republican Party.
Focusing their *xenophobia* on *Catholics* who formed
a large proportion of the surging *Irish & German* segment of
the population, the Know-Nothings got their name
from their policy of denying any knowledge
of their clandestine anti-immigrant activities.
Former President *Millard Fillmore* would garner
over 21% of the popular vote as a third party candidate
in the election of 1856,
but after that the American party splintered
over the issue of slavery and its members
would retreat into the Democratic and Republican parties.

"I don't know if you've ever been to Kansas,
but it really hardly seems worth fighting over."

"Have you ever seen the Wizard of Oz?"
"I've never seen anywhere so bleak. "
"If I were Dorothy,
I would have just let the witch keep those stupid slippers
and stayed in Oz."

In an effort to straddle the controversial issue of slavery that
was threatening to divide the country once and for all,
popular sovereignty arose as a democratic solution
to the divisive problem.
While the concept of majority rule is certainly consistent
with US history, a fear arose that pro-slavery advocates would
flood into new territories and legitimize slavery even as
the rapidly-expanding popular sentiment
in most of the nation opposed it.
The *Kansas-Nebraska Act* of 1854 would provide the spark
that would ignite the controversy.
Needing the support of southern Democrats in Congress
to authorize a *transcontinental railroad* terminating in his
native Illinois, Senator *Stephen Douglas* proposed legislation
that would open all territories to popular sovereignty, even
those north of the 36°30' boundary previously decided
by the Missouri Compromise of 1820.
Not even Douglas foresaw how incendiary
the impact of the legislation would be.

"Let's get a move on;
I haven't killed anyone yet today and I've still got planting to do."

The violence among Americans finally came to a head
as a consequence of the Kansas-Nebraska Act.
"Border ruffians" from neighboring Missouri flooded into
Kansas and established a pro-slavery legislature in *Lecompton*.
Anti-slavery advocates funded by the
New England Emigrant Aid Company
did the same for their side at *Topeka*.
Two free-soilers were murdered when the anti-slavery town of
Lawrence was attacked in 1856. Abolitionists led by
John Brown would retaliate by killing five pro-slavery settlers
at *Pottawatomie Creek*. Chaos ensued when a rigged vote was
held in which both options for a proposed state constitution
allowed for slavery. Abolitionist voters boycotted the vote, and
the Constitution guaranteeing the existence of slavery
was ratified overwhelmingly.
Even popular sovereignty champion Stephen Douglas
recognized the chicanery of the election
and Congress rejected Kansas' application for statehood.
Kansas would not become a state until the secession of 11 states
would facilitate Kansas' recognition as a free state.

*"It's my understanding that vertical stripes
are slimming;
I'd hate to be fat-shamed
by that donkey the Democrats hired."*

Picking up members from former Whigs, Free-Soilers,
Know-Nothings, & northern Democrats, a new party burst on
the national scene in the presidential election of 1856.
The *Republican* Party would call for repeal of both
the Fugitive Slave law and the Kansas-Nebraska Act,
for free homesteads for settlers, for an increased tariff to protect
manufacturers and for no further expansion of slavery.
Mexican War hero *John C. Fremont* would run against
Democrat James Buchanan and win 11 of the 16 free states,
a remarkable showing for a brand-new coalition.
Starting with the election of *Abraham Lincoln* in 1860,
Republicans would dominate the presidency
in all but four elections prior to 1932.

"When is somebody going to invent Advil, already?"

The deteriorating national discourse over the slavery issue
came to a head in 1856 when Senator *Charles Sumner*
of Massachusetts delivered a blistering attack in his speech
"The Crime Against Kansas."
Sumner would viciously attack the character and intelligence
of popular South Carolina Senator Andrew Butler, and Butler's
cousin Representative *Preston Brooks* avenged this slight
by approaching Sumner on the floor of the Senate
and beating him senseless with a cane.
Sumner was so badly injured that he could not serve
for three years, a period of time during which he was re-elected
by Massachusetts and his seat left empty
as witness to southern barbarism.
Brooks would resign his seat after censure by the House, but
would be enthusiastically re-elected by his district at home.
The fight on the Senate floor would soon pale
in comparison to the violence to come.

Possibly no single incident would more directly contribute
to the eventual war between the states than
the Supreme Court's 1857 ruling in *Dred Scott v. Sandford.*
Dred Scott, a Missouri slave had sued for his freedom based on
the fact that his owner had taken him to the Wisconsin
territory in which slavery was illegal per both
the *Northwest Ordinance of 1787* and the
Missouri Compromise.
Chief Justice *Roger Taney*, writing for the majority,
rejected Scott's suit, arguing that Scott had no status to bring
suit as the Constitution did not recognize
African-Americans as citizens;
That Congress had no right to disallow slavery in any territories;
& that therefore the Constitutionally-guaranteed
right to property could not be abridged except by state law
once a territory entered the union.
Taney's ruling invalidated the Missouri Compromise and
opened all western territories up to slavery,
outraging abolitionists and free-soilers alike
and setting the stage for the Civil War soon to come.

"I appreciate the warning about the house,
but would it have killed him to speak up about the scaffolding?"

Abraham Lincoln would emerge onto the national stage
in 1858 as the Republican candidate vying against
Democrat *Stephen Douglas* for
Douglas' Senate seat representing Illinois.
In a series of debates, Lincoln articulated his position that
"a house divided against itself cannot stand,"
implying that the nation could not go forward
half slave-owning and half free.
Douglas would win the election, but would alienate
Southern Democrats who decried his *Freeport Doctrine* which
stated that slavery could be restricted in territories that failed
to affirmatively pass legislation protecting it,
contravening the Dred Scott decision.
This "betrayal" perceived by southern Democrats would cost
Douglas in the presidential election of 1860
and allow Lincoln to win that election even though
he wouldn't appear on ballots throughout the South.

"I regret that I have but one life to give for my country."

"If you strike me down, I shall become more powerful than you can possibly imagine."

"Dammit; all the good speeches are already taken."
"Just get it over with, already."

In October of 1859,
radical abolitionist *John Brown* and a group of followers
attacked a federal arsenal at *Harper's Ferry*, Virginia.
Brown envisioned utilizing the weapons from the armory
to equip local slaves and leading this army of liberated slaves
from plantation to plantation,
bringing about an end to the scourge of slavery.
Brown's attack was quickly foiled by federal troops under the
command of *Robert E. Lee*, and after a two-day siege,
Brown and his followers were captured.
Brown would be convicted and executed,
but would become a powerful icon of the abolitionist movement
and the most reviled example of the existential threat
to the way of life of the southern slaveholders.

"If I had known how this was going to turn out for me,
I would have voted for one of the other guys."

"Who even cares whose picture is on the penny, anyway?"

Never would the United States see a presidential election more divisive than in 1860. *Abraham Lincoln* would run on behalf of the Republicans, opposing the expansion of slavery but not calling for its abolition.

Stephen Douglas would run for the northern bloc of a broken Democratic Party, advocating popular sovereignty and enforcement of the Fugitive Slave Law.

John C. Breckinridge would champion southern Democrats who called for expansion of slavery throughout all territories as well as the annexation of Cuba, where slavery could further flourish.

Finally, *John Bell* ran as the candidate of a new *Constitutional Union Party* that pledged adherence to the Constitution and the preservation of the Union.

With the fractured vote, Lincoln was able to carry the north and the west and be elected president with 59% of the electoral votes but not even 40% of the popular vote.

Following Lincoln's election, South Carolina, Georgia, Alabama, Mississippi, Florida, Louisiana & Texas seceded and in February of 1861 formed the *Confederate States of America*.

Lame-duck President *James Buchanan* did nothing in the face of this secession, and the nation would anxiously await what would transpire with Lincoln's inauguration.

"When they said 'shots all around'
I thought something entirely different was going on."

"DUCK!!!"

On April 12th, 1861,
Confederate batteries fired the first shots of the
American Civil War on *Fort Sumter* in Charleston harbor.
The fort had been held by the US military since South Carolina's
secession but sorely needed to be resupplied.
President Lincoln was insistent on not initiating hostilities
with the Confederacy, but it was his decision to attempt
the resupplying of the fort by sea that provoked
the Confederate Army to attack.
A garrison under the command of Major Robert Anderson
withstood a 34 hour siege but then had to surrender the fort
to the Confederate Army.

*If Robert E. Lee hadn't suffered so badly from
carpal tunnel syndrome,
the Anaconda Plan wouldn't have stood a chance.*

Aged military hero *Winfield Scott* was given command
of the Union forces at the outset of the war
after Robert E. Lee had resigned his commission when
Virginia, Arkansas, North Carolina, & Tennessee
joined the Confederacy after the attack on Fort Sumter.
Scott developed the Union strategy that came to be known
as the *Anaconda Plan*, which consisted of:
Blockading southern ports to choke off trade and supplies;
Seizing control of the Mississippi River
to bisect the Confederacy; &
Capturing the new Confederate capital
at Richmond, Virginia.
Although ultimately the goals would all be realized,
it would take four long years of death and destruction
for Scott's plan to ultimately lead the Union to victory.

"The battle sure didn't turn out like we expected;
there's just something sketchy about this…"

The tone of the early years of the war would be set
at the *First Battle of Bull Run*.
Although the Union had a 4:1 advantage in population,
an overwhelming advantage in financial, transportation, &
manufacturing resources, & a strong central government in
place, the South possessed superior military leadership and
only had to defend itself as opposed to the North which had to
conquer the rebellious states. The First Battle of Bull Run
dashed the Union hopes for a quick and easy victory
when a larger Union force was forced to retreat
in the face of an aggressive maneuver executed by
General Thomas "Stonewall" Jackson.
The Confederate victory would delude the South
that the war would be easily won,
but served to shock the North into the realization
that a total mobilization of the nation's strength
would be required to win what many consider
to be the world's first truly ***"modern war."***

"Knock-knock."

"Who's there?"

"Time."

"Time who?"

"Time to attack, you moron!
You're going to be late to your own funeral at the rate you're going!"

After a year of Confederate battlefield successes,
President Lincoln entrusted command of the Union Army
to General *George McClellan*.
"Tardy George" was beloved by his troops for the consideration
he showed them, but his reluctance to commit his army to battle
rankled the president.
In March of 1862 McClellan finally initiated
the *Peninsular Campaign* but his attack on the Virginia capital
was stymied by General Lee's defense and after five months
a frustrated Lincoln replaced McClellan as commander.
McClellan would get a second chance at command
but would again be dismissed after failing
to press his advantage after the Battle of Antietam.
McClellan would surface a final time as Lincoln's
Democratic opponent in the presidential election of 1864,
where he would yet again demonstrate
his inability to achieve victory.

This all happened because a Confederate officer
wanted to keep his cigars dry
so he wrapped them in Lee's battle plans
and then they fell out of his pocket.
See kids? Smoking really does kill.

September of 1862 would see the tide turn in the war.
Lee capitalized on his momentum by planning an attack
at *Antietam* Creek in Maryland,
hopeful that a crushing victory in a Union state
might convince foreign nations to provide aid
to the Confederacy. When apprised of the attack once a
copy of Lee's plans fell into his hands, McClellan successfully
repelled the attack in what would become the bloodiest day
of the entire war. Frustrated that McClellan failed to pursue Lee
as he retreated back to Virginia, Lincoln relieved him
of command once and for all. In addition to forestalling foreign
recognition and aid for the Confederacy,
the Union victory gave Lincoln
the opportunity to issue the *Emancipation Proclamation*

Although Lincoln had expressed that if he could
save the Union by freeing all of the slaves,
by freeing none of them,
or by freeing some of them but not others,
as of January 1st, 1863
Lincoln committed to freeing all slaves
still held in rebellious states.
Lincoln's hesitancy regarding emancipation
in no small way reflected his concern that the five
"border states" of **Missouri, Kentucky, Maryland, Delaware**
and the newly-created *West Virginia* might swing
toward the Confederacy if he eradicated slavery
by presidential fiat.
In reality, the *Emancipation Proclamation* freed slaves in areas
where Lincoln lacked the capacity to do so
and did not free slaves in areas in which he did.
Nevertheless, the Emancipation Proclamation
broadened the appeal of the Union cause
amongst abolitionists both foreign and domestic.

"Thanks a lot, Abe;
now generations of kids are going to lose points on a test
because they don't know how many years a 'score' is."

Realizing that the superior resources of the Union
likely made their victory inevitable,
Lee decided to foray one last surge into Union territory
on July 1st, 1863.
The three-day *Battle of Gettysburg*
would be the war's bloodiest
with over 50,000 combined casualties.
Although Lee would escape, for the remainder of the war
the Confederate Army would be on the defensive
and the Union victory stiffened northern resolve
to pursue the war to its bitter end,
the unconditional surrender of the Confederacy.

"But President Lincoln, Grant is a drunk!"

"Then get a barrel of whatever he drinks to my other generals; the man wins!"

Having dominated the Confederacy in the west
including gaining control of the Mississippi River
following the successful siege of *Vicksburg*,
General *Ulysses S. Grant* was given overall control
of the Army of the Potomac.
Grant's willingness to wage a ruthless *war of attrition*
led to a succession of victories that visited the horrors of war
upon not only the Confederate military,
but on the entirety of the Southern population.
Grant would win victories
in the Wilderness Campaign, Spotsylvania & Cold Harbor
at great cost, but his relentless pursuit of
Lee's Army of Northern Virginia
would ultimately prove effective.

Sherman's
"Tango to the Mountains"
didn't get nearly
the attention as his
"March to the Sea."

While Grant was slowly tightening the noose around Lee
in Northern Virginia,
General *William Tecumseh Sherman* was
visiting death and destruction upon the deep South.
Sherman marched inexorably from Tennessee to Georgia,
leaving a 20 mile-wide swath of destruction
in his army's wake.
Sherman burned Atlanta in September,
buttressing Lincoln's re-election chances;
presented the newly re-elected president with Savannah
as a Christmas gift; and then headed north to devastate
South Carolina, the initiator of the horrible war.
Sherman's March to the Sea not only destroyed
his Confederate adversaries,
more importantly it broke the will of the southern people.

"In all honesty, the war has left me pretty exhausted,

but if the show is really as good as you're saying,

then sure, I'll take your theater tickets."

"I hope that it's funny;

I need more drama like I need a hole in the head."

The war would finally end with Lee's surrender
on April 9th, 1865 at *Appomattox Court House*, Virginia.
Grant was magnanimous in his victory,
allowing Lee and his soldiers to return home
with their horses and supplies.
President Lincoln, who had never recognized
the legitimacy of the secession,
looked forward to welcoming back the wayward states
of the Confederacy on the most generous of terms.
Unfortunately for all, Lincoln's stance
as a powerful voice for reconciliation
would be silenced on April 14th
when embittered Confederate sympathizer
John Wilkes Booth
shot and killed President Lincoln
as he watched a play at Ford's Theater in Washington.

"If you can manage to put the Union back together,
I've got a friend who I think is going to need your help ..."

Prior to his assassination, President Lincoln had advocated for a *reconstruction* plan that issued pardons for most Confederates who accepted the end of slavery and pledged their allegiance to the United States and allowed for the rehabilitation of any state in which 10% of voters took an oath of loyalty.

When Vice President **Andrew Johnson** took over as president, he additionally disenfranchised all Confederate office-holders and high-ranking military leaders as well as the wealthiest Southerners in possession of $20,000 or more of property.

As President, Johnson, a Tennessee Democrat who had remained loyal during the war, regularly vetoed congressional legislation protecting the rights of the newly-freed former slaves. *"Radical Republicans"* led by *Thaddeus Stevens & Charles Sumner* blocked Johnson's plans and implemented *military reconstruction* that treated the South as conquered territory, ruled by Union generals under martial law.

"Free at last, free at last, thank God almighty I'm free at last!"

"It's amazing that things can get so much better
and still be so bad."

A crucial component of the congressional reconstruction plan
was the ratification of three amendments to the Constitution
that would protect the newly-freed African Americans
from future legislation that might restrict their rights should
Southern congressmen, who would gain 11 seats
in the House of Representatives with the *3/5 Compromise*
now invalidated, ever rally support to oppress the former slaves.
The *13th Amendment* banned slavery;
The *14th Amendment* granted all rights of citizenship; &
The *15th Amendment* granted adult Black males voting rights.
Ratification of these amendments was made a condition of the
11 states of the Confederacy regaining their status in the Union.

"You think we're acting childish?
You should see how Congress and the President
are getting along; we look like angels."

During his single term in office,
Andrew Johnson issued 29 vetoes,
surpassing the total of all previous presidents.
In an effort to gain support, Johnson toured the nation prior to
the midterm elections of 1866, but his efforts backfired and
a veto-proof majority of legislators
ran roughshod over the president.
Tensions would boil over when Johnson fired
Secretary of War *Edwin Stanton*, a Republican undermining
him in his own cabinet, in violation of the *Tenure of Office Act*,
which (unconstitutionally) stipulated that the Senate
had to confirm any firings from the president's cabinet.
Johnson became the first president ever *impeached*,
charged with 11 "high crimes & misdemeanors"
and ultimately acquitted by a single vote.
A chastened Johnson would finish his term quietly,
with the Republican Congress firmly in control.

"I wish you and your hoe the best of luck."

In the midst of the war, there would be several significant pieces of legislation unrelated to the conflict that are worth noting. The *Homestead Act of 1862* offered *160 acres of free land* in the Great Plains to any settler that farmed the land for at least five years. This act encouraged settlement and gave even the poorest Americans at least the hope of a fresh start.

"Let's be honest;
if it weren't for football and partying,
most of us wouldn't be interested in these schools."

"Still, those were nine of the best years of my life."

The *Morrill Land Grant Act of 1862*
provided land for states to sell in order to utilize the profits
to endow state universities focused on
agriculture, engineering & mining.
These affordable institutions of higher education would
foster tremendous advancements going forward,
enriching both the economic and social fabric of society.

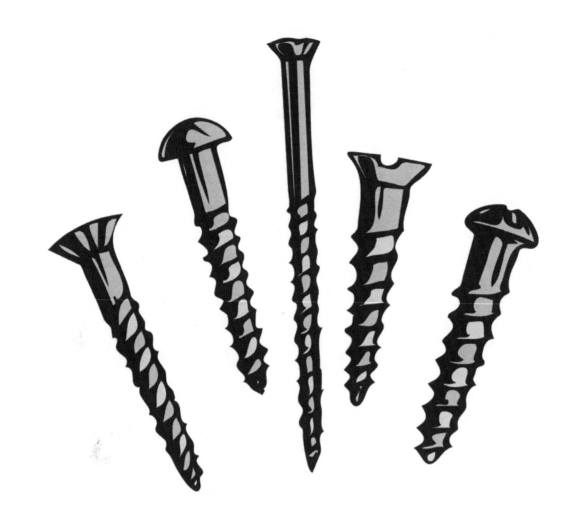

Southern strategy for the newly emancipated slaves

after the Compromise of 1877

Despite having started out so optimistically,
Reconstruction would begin to lose its political support
long before it could fulfill its promise to uplift the former slaves.
When conflicting electoral ballots from
South Carolina, Louisiana & Florida
made the winner of the presidential election of 1876 unclear,
a specially-empaneled electoral commission made up of
eight Republicans and seven Democrats reached a decision
known as the *Compromise of 1877.*
Republican *Rutherford B. Hayes* became president,
but in exchange Reconstruction ended and the troops
that had endeavored to protect African American rights
in the South were withdrawn, leaving 4,000,000 former slaves
at the mercy of a vengeful and powerful white majority.

Even before the end of Reconstruction,
racist southern governments implemented restrictions
on the ostensibly free former slaves.
Black Codes restricted property ownership,
required Blacks to present passes to be in certain areas,
prevented testimony in court against whites, &
required proof of employment or risk arrest for vagrancy.
The 13th Amendment allowed for "involuntary servitude"
as punishment for a crime, and many African Americans
soon found themselves no better off
than they had been before the war.

"Unless that mule is invisible,
I think we're getting the short end of the stick again."

While the war had facilitated their freedom for the former slaves, they were provided with virtually nothing else. The *Freedmen's Bureau* did teach approximately 200,000 Blacks how to read, but as farmers with no land or supplies, the former slaves soon found themselves having to contract themselves to their former owners as *sharecroppers*. A typical arrangement consisted of African Americans providing labor on the land of the former owners, using tools and resources provided by the owner. Profits would be split 50/50, but many sharecroppers would find themselves unable to leave due to debts they had accrued prior to the harvest. A Republican promise of *"40 acres and a mule"* for each former slave family never came to fruition, and generations of African Americans would find life not much different after the war from what it had been before.

"Then charge them a tax,
and if that doesn't stop them, give them a literacy test;
And then disqualify them if their grandfather couldn't vote."

"If you're not as white as this page,
I don't want you to vote, got it?"

Prior to the end of Reconstruction,
14 African American Congressmen & 2 Senators
would be elected to serve from the states
of the former Confederacy. The rapid and systematic
disenfranchisement of Black voters almost completely
eliminated the right of citizens to vote their say in their own
governance for which the Revolutionary War had ostensibly
been fought. A variety of tactics would deny African Americans
their equal right to vote for the better part of the next century.
Among these outrages were:
Poll taxes that required payment in order to vote;
Literacy tests that unfairly discriminated against Blacks
who had been forbidden to learn how to read; &
"Grandfather clauses" which mandated that in order to vote,
one's grandfather had to have been eligible to vote.

Until we have justice for everyone,
we don't have justice for anyone.

As if being robbed of one's rights weren't bad enough,
in the years between Reconstruction and the
Civil Rights Era of the 1960's,
3,446 African Americans
would be hanged by violent racist mobs.
Often for no other reason than for having tried to vote,
open a business, or for having spoken out against injustice,
Blacks throughout the country but overwhelmingly in the South
found themselves harassed, tortured or murdered.
Lynch mobs could be organized by racist groups,
most notably the *Ku Klux Klan*
founded in 1867 by Nathan Bedford Forrest,
or simply emerge quickly and organically
from groups of embittered southern whites
who resented the possibility of Black equality.

"I'm just nuts about agriculture."

(Sorry; I couldn't resist.)

One of the great heroes to emerge out of the disaster
that was Reconstruction was *George Washington Carver*.
Carver would be the first Black student
to attend Iowa State University,
one of the Land-Grant colleges created by the Morrill Act,
and would earn Bachelor's & Master's degrees
in botany and agricultural sciences.
Invited by *Booker T. Washington*
to *Tuskegee Institute* in 1896,
Carver would head its Agriculture Department for 47 years.
During that span, Carver's innovations regarding *crop rotation*
and *soil rejuvenation* saved agriculture in the South,
where nutrients in the soil had been depleted by decades
of cotton and tobacco farming. Carver proved that crops such as
peanuts and sweet potatoes could not only
replenish the nitrogen leached from the soil
but could provide a commercially viable
source of nutrition and income.

"Oh my God; stop the horses!"

"We're about to run into a bison on the next page!"

Continuing a tradition that had been evident
since the establishment of the
first English settlements along the Atlantic seaboard,
settlers moved inexorably westward
in search of fortune and opportunity.
Although the Pacific states of *California* & *Oregon*
would flourish initially, as the 19th century drew toward its
close the *Great Plains* beckoned, and even the last
"Indian Territory"
that had been set aside would be taken over when *Oklahoma*
was opened to white settlement on April 22nd, 1889
when over 50,000 *"Sooners"* rushed in to claim homesteads.
Settlers came by foot, *Conestoga* wagon,
and eventually by train, imposing "civilized" ways-of-life
on the *"Great American Desert."*

"How about you drop that gun
and then we'll see just how tough you are, cowboy…"

As more and more Native American tribes were forced away
from their ancestral lands toward the interior of the continent,
many of those on the Great Plains adapted to their new habitat
by relying on herds of *bison*
numbering in the hundreds of thousands.
Having mastered a nomadic lifestyle
following the introduction of horses by the Spanish,
numerous tribes hunted the bison for meat and hides,
providing them with what should have been
an inexhaustible resource.
As American settlers headed west,
millions of these powerful animals were slain
by hunters hired by the railroads and by ranchers
seeking pastureland on which to graze cattle.
By the turn of the century,
the largest land mammal in the Americas
was threatened with extinction.
By the late 20th century, conservation and commercial efforts
to raise bison had thankfully saved the powerful animal
for future generations to appreciate.

"Maybe it would have been a good idea
if somebody would have invented the tetanus shot first;
these things get rusty fast!"

As ranchers settled the Plains the prairie grasses
sustained everyone's herds and *cowboys*,
many Mexican or African American,
would tend the animals and eventually lead them
on long cattle-drives to stockyards
where trains could ship the animals east.
As years passed, farmers moved west and found themselves
in competition with the ranchers whose herds
would destroy the crops planted
where the grasses had previously flourished.
The invention and mass production of *barbed wire*
by *Joseph Glidden* would provide farmers with
a cheap and effective way of protecting their crops
from cattle, and end the days of the *"open range"*
which so many associate with the "wild, wild west."

"I thought you brought the drinks."

"No; I brought the gold spike.
You were supposed to bring the drinks."

"Who's going to tell hundreds of Irish workers
that we don't have any drinks?"

"I know, right? When's the first train out of here?"

Between 1862 & 1893,
five *transcontinental railroads* would be constructed
linking the Atlantic & Pacific coasts.
The *Union Pacific* & *Central Pacific* met on May 10th, 1869
at *Promontory Point, Utah*.
Largely built by *Irish* and *Chinese* immigrant workers,
the railroad connected
Omaha, Nebraska & Sacramento, California.
Over the next 24 years, the Northern Pacific, Southern Pacific,
the Atchison, Topeka, & Santa Fe and the Great Northern lines
would link east and west providing a surplus of connectivity
that would lead to competition and consolidation
between different railroads, and financial instability
for speculators who had invested
in what was to become America's largest industry.

"We're the US Cavalry;
They're a bunch of heathen savages;
So what if they outnumber us 10:1?"

"Let's get this party started; what could go wrong?"

Rivaling slavery as the greatest injustice perpetrated
by the United States upon fellow Americans,
the treatment of Native Americans has almost without
exception been one of betrayal and tragedy.
Treaties signed at *Fort Laramie* & *Fort Atkinson* in 1851
had set aside large *reservations* for the Plains Indians.
Over the next few decades, however, as land and resources
became desirable and the West became more easily accessible,
the treaties were broken repeatedly
and a series of *Indian Wars*
led to the devastation of America's first peoples.
The *Indian Appropriation Act of 1871* ended US recognition
of distinct tribes, and by the time of *Custer's Last Stand*
at the *Battle of Little Bighorn* in 1876
and the capture of *Chief Joseph* in 1877,
the era of even quasi-independence
for Native Americans had ended.

A lot more than knees were wounded, unfortunately.

The end of the Indian Wars took place in 1890
at the *Battle of Wounded Knee*.
200 Indian American men, women & children
were massacred on the Dakota Territory
having put their faith in the *Ghost Dance*,
a religiously-inspired ritual that maintained
that a rejection of all things associated
with white society would make the Native Americans
irresistible in battle and would allow them
to overcome their adversaries.
The era of resistance would end and generations
of forced assimilation would ensue,
with Native American children
sent to boarding schools where their culture
was shunned and "American" ways reinforced.
The *Dawes Severalty Act of 1887* broke up tribal lands,
allotting 160 acres to Indian families and US citizenship
if they maintained their plots for 25 years.
Although 47,000,000 acres were distributed,
90,000,000 acres were kept by the government
for itself or for sale to speculators.
By 1900, there would be only 200,000 Native Americans left.

"What kind of road trip are they even on?"
"There won't be a 7-Eleven here for 150 years;
who's gonna travel across the whole dang country
without a Big Gulp and some Doritos?"

"And they call us savages."

In 1890, the US Census Bureau declared
that the frontier was no more,
with settlement covering virtually all regions of the United
States. Historian *Frederick Jackson Turner*
suggested that the end of the frontier signaled a change
in the nation's history, which had always encouraged
bold strides into the unknown.
Turner suggested in his *Frontier Thesis*
that the "safety valve" that the frontier had always presented
had offered endless opportunities for second chances,
and had cultivated in the American people a sense of
rugged individualism and respect for democracy.
It is perhaps due to the loss of this frontier
that as the century turned, the United States
would begin to look outward beyond our coasts
for future opportunities for growth and influence.

"Don't worry; there's like zero chance of this getting out of control and causing a wildfire that rages over hundreds of miles."

"What do you think; that it's 2021 or something?"

Not all Americans sought to exploit
the wide-open spaces of the West.
Yellowstone National Park in Wyoming
would be established in 1872 as the first of what
would become hundreds of federally-maintained
parks, forests, coastlines, & national monuments.
Millions of acres of land would be conserved
for our nation's posterity thanks to the efforts of
preservationists ranging from *John Muir*, founder of
the *Sierra Club*, to President *Theodore Roosevelt*.
Whether we will choose to continue our stewardship
of our nation's resources will determine
whether our "purple mountains' majesty"
will continue to awe future generations of Americans.

Gentlemen: You have undertaken to cheat me.

I won't sue you, for the law is too slow.

I'll ruin you.

Yours truly, Cornelius Vanderbilt

As manufacturing began to dominate the US economy during the mid-1800's, wealthy industrialists known as *Robber Barons* began to concentrate wealth and power to a heretofore unimaginable degree. *Cornelius Vanderbilt*, the owner of a successful steamship line, saw the potential for dominating the railroads. *"The Commodore"* would become one of the *Gilded Age's* wealthiest men thanks to his control of the railways, most prominently the *New York Central* line. Vanderbilt helped to popularize *standard gauge & steel rails*, both of which streamlined America's transportation network. Vanderbilt utilized *cutthroat competition*, but in the end was very philanthropic with his fortune which reached $105,000,000 at his death, the equivalent to nearly $2.8 billion today.

"A free trip to Chicago?"

"And it's all air-conditioned?"

"Where do I sign up; this prairie is for the birds."

Meat became a cheaper and more significant portion
of the typical American's daily menu
thanks to the innovations of *Gustavus Swift*.
Prior to the late 1800's, cattle had to be herded
from the Southwest to railheads such as Kansas City
to be loaded on stock cars and shipped alive to the East.
The cattle would lose much of their weight and their value
being herded distances that could exceed 1,000 miles.
Many cattle arrived sickly or dead, and 60% of the animal
wasn't even fit for human consumption.
Swift pioneered the butchering of meat in slaughterhouses
nearer to the Plains, and then the shipment of "dressed" meat
in *refrigerated boxcars* with virtually no waste at all.
Swift was also instrumental in finding productive uses for the
other parts of the slaughtered animals, such as adhesives, hides,
& fertilizers. By the time of his death in 1903,
Swift's meatpacking plants were processing
8,000,000 cattle, hogs & sheep every year.

"Watson; come here, I want to see you."

"What do you mean, 'wrong number?'"

"I just invented this thing; there <u>aren't</u> any other numbers!"

1876 would see the invention of the *telephone*
by *Alexander Graham Bell*.
Bell was inspired to research sound in an effort to ameliorate
the deafness of his mother and his wife.
Following Samuel Morse's invention of the telegraph by
30 years, Bell's invention expanded near-instantaneous
communication to everyone, given that it conveyed the spoken
word and not *Morse Code* signals that needed to be deciphered
by a professional telegrapher. Bell's first message to his assistant
Thomas Watson was "Watson; come here, I want to see you."
By 1886, there would be 150,000 telephones in the United States
and by 1915 transcontinental cables linked New York
and San Francisco over a span of 3,400 miles.

"This process blows."

"Indeed."

English inventor *Henry Bessemer* is responsible for an
invention that led to steel becoming America's
most important product.
In 1856 Bessemer perfected a method of blowing cold oxygen
across molten iron to remove its impurities.
The *Bessemer Process* was quicker, easier and cheaper
than the steelmaking processes which predated it,
and made the production of steel
the cornerstone of America's *industrial revolution.*
Steel was stronger and lighter than iron,
and would facilitate great advancements
in transportation, construction and industry.

*"I don't care what the Supreme Court says;
D'you know what kind of integration America is ready for?"*

"Vertical Integration."

*"Buy the ore; buy the coal; buy the railroads; buy the foundries;
buy the wholesalers. Buy it all."*

*"Then call JP and see if he has any loose change sitting around;
Maybe, oh-I don't know, about $400,000,000."*

Andrew Carnegie immigrated to the United States from Scotland as a young boy with very few resources other than a bright mind and a willingness to work hard in order to succeed. Carnegie's drive and aptitude would be recognized early, as he moved from a job as a "bobbin-boy" in a textile factory earning $1.20/week to a telegrapher to a secretary and eventually a superintendent for the Pennsylvania Railroad. Under the guidance of his boss who encouraged the young Carnegie to make use of his personal library, Carnegie began investing and would ultimately parlay his investments into ownership of *Carnegie Steel*, which by 1889 would lead the US to become the world's largest producer of steel. While Carnegie did not invent steel-making, he did implement a new organizational strategy that revolutionized its production. *Vertical Integration* allowed Carnegie to insulate his company from cost exposure by controlling each stage of the production process, from raw materials to transportation to production to sales. In 1889 Carnegie published *The Gospel of Wealth* in which he asserted that the wealthy had a moral obligation to use their good fortune for the betterment of society. Carnegie would sell his company to *JP Morgan* in 1901, who would form it into *US Steel*, the world's first billion-dollar corporation. The sale made Carnegie the world's richest man, and he donated much of his fortune to institutions that would enable others to better themselves as he had, including universities and, most notably, several thousand *public libraries*.

"I know, I know;
but it definitely doesn't say anything about
undercutting the competition,
even if it's your own brother, does it?"

"Or establishing a monopoly that controls 97%
of the oil-refining capacity of the United States, does it?"

"Then I'm all good.
Now hit the road; I have a Sunday-school class to teach."

Carnegie would retain his status as the wealthiest man
in the world for seven years. He would ultimately be surpassed
by another self-made tycoon, ***John D. Rockefeller***.
An austere puritanical businessman, Rockefeller felt that
his success was evidence of God's favor.
As *kerosene* became the nation's fuel source for lighting
in the mid-1800's, Rockefeller's ***Standard Oil Company***
would utilize the strategy of *Horizontal Integration*
to eventually monopolize 97% of the nation's
oil-refining capacity. Standard Oil would undercut the prices of
its competitors until they went bankrupt,
and then swoop in and buy their companies.
While Standard Oil did indeed dominate the market,
it also brought a quality product to consumers
at rock-bottom prices. As time passed, Standard Oil
ran afoul of the antitrust sentiments of the early 20th century
and would be forced to break up into seven different companies
in an effort to foster competition.
Rockefeller would emerge from this even wealthier
than he had been before,
and both his wealth and his philanthropy
would endure to the present day.

"Whose bright idea was this, anyway?"

"Oh, that's right; it was mine."

*"Quick; someone grab one of my motion picture cameras
and go film Tesla and Westinghouse
fighting over second place."*

Perhaps no inventor has been more highly-regarded than "The Wizard of Menlo Park" *Thomas Edison*. Edison's legacy would include 1,093 patents for inventions ranging from the *phonograph*, the *movie camera*, a practical and long-lasting *filament* for the *electric light bulb*, and for *Direct Current (DC)* for powering America's cities. Eventually, after losing business to George Westinghouse's *Alternating Current (AC)*, Edison Electric would be sold to financier *JP Morgan* who would combine it with rival companies to form *General Electric*, which would dominate its field into the 21st century.

"Horatio Alger had better be right;
If I climb all the way to the top of this mountain
and there isn't a piece of the American pie up there,
he and I are going to have a major problem."

The accomplishments of self-made men such as
Carnegie, Rockefeller & Edison formed the inspiration
for one of the most prolific authors of the late 1800's.
Horatio Alger wrote stories that reflected
the ***Puritan work ethic*** and which sold millions of copies.
Alger's more than 100 books, the most famous of which was
Ragged Dick, followed a distinct formula in which
a kindly and successful benefactor would befriend a young boy
and mentor him, and thanks to this help
and the boy's own initiative and hard work,
the boy would triumph over adversity and become a success.
Alger's legacy is significantly tainted by the revelation of his
own inappropriate relationships with youth that forced him
to leave the ministry and turn to writing as a vocation.

"Not to be too cynical, but a little less 'wealth' and a lot more 'gospel' might have led to a significantly better outcome."

The end of the 19th and beginning of the 20th centuries would come to be known as the *"Gilded Age,"* a term coined by quintessential American author and social commentator *Mark Twain* to describe how the superficially grand and affluent appearance of American society disguised a United States in which the disparity between the elite and the common people was enormous. Tycoons such as Vanderbilt, Rockefeller & Morgan lived like royalty while the overwhelming number of Americans subsisted on mere dollars a week. Although huge divisions still remain between America's wealthiest individuals and the majority of the population, a recognition of the danger of the accumulation of so much wealth in the hands of so few people has led to reforms that have lessened the disparity over the years.

"Amazon, schmamazon;"
"Nothing will ever have the impact upon mass-merchandising
that a catalog the size of a phone book will."
"What's that? What's a phone book?"
"Sigh…"

America's surging manufacturing capacity was kept busy
satisfying the demand of the nation's
increasingly acquisitive population.
Innovations in marketing and transportation would facilitate
the establishment of nation-wide retailers such as
Montgomery Ward and *Sears, Roebuck & Company*.
Sears in particular would dominate the retail market,
supplementing hundreds of retail locations
with catalog sales that dwarfed all other competitors.
The Sears catalog was shipped to virtually all American homes
and contained every imaginable item
ranging from farm tools to toiletries to entire houses
that would be shipped via
the nation's omnipresent railroad system.

Structural steel?
✓

Elevators?
✓

Air-conditioning?
✓

Revolving doors?
✓

"Whaddya mean
you can't find the keys?"

"Grrr…"

The introduction of *street-cars*, pulled initially by horses but ultimately powered by electricity, would allow cities to expand outward and for the wealthy to move away from urban centers to more pastoral suburbs. In spite of this, the growing urban population fueled by massive influxes in immigration and former farmworkers seeking employment pushed the capacity of cities to the extreme. America's cities began to expand upward in addition to outward.

Chicago's *Home Insurance Building* is generally considered to be the world's first skyscraper, built in 1885 and stretching ten stories toward the sky. Unlike prior masonry buildings, the Home Insurance Building utilized a curtain wall system supported by a *steel skeleton*. Innovations such as *elevators* to obviate an arduous climb, *air conditioning* to make practicable interior rooms devoid of windows, and *revolving doors* to prevent conditioned air from escaping the building were crucial to the successful utilization of these new structures. While many structures were grand, *"dumbbell tenements"* became the bane of many poor inhabitants, with poor ventilation due to air shafts that provided inadequate airflow and they became fire hazards due to poor sanitation. Health hazards such as typhoid and cholera would lead cities to introduce *treated water* and *modern sewer systems* to enable the concentration of so many people into such congested circumstances.

"I know it sounds good,
but you might want to take that whole
'huddled masses yearning to breathe free'
part with a grain of salt."

The *Chinese Exclusion Act of 1882*
was a crystal-clear example of the nativist resentment
embraced by many Americans who were becoming
increasingly suspicious of the skyrocketing immigration rates
that characterized the United States at the turn of the century.
Still the only immigration law ever passed in the US
that exclusively targeted a single nationality,
the Chinese Exclusion Act would be but the first of several
attempts by American *xenophobes* to keep the United States
a nation dominated by white Protestants.
It would not be until 1943 that the law would be modified,
even then allowing only 105 Chinese nationals per year
to immigrate to the United States.

"Well, you're definitely not a huddled mass,
but are you tired, poor & yearning to breathe free?"
"If so, let me help you."

As poor immigrants flooded America's shores in the late 1800's coming primarily from Southern and Eastern European regions and lacking a connection to previous immigrant populations from Ireland, Germany and the rest of Northwestern Europe, *settlement houses* arose in response to their needs. Inspired by the *"social gospel"* espoused primarily by white Protestant ladies of America's new *middle-class*, the settlement houses sought to bring the new immigrants lessons and skills that would help to acculturate them to their new home. *Hull House* in Chicago was built in 1889 by *Jane Addams* and brought teachers of English, job skills and home economics to the inner city where the immigrant populations resided. The settlement houses would lead to the introduction of *social work* as a vocation, and Jane Addams would become the first woman ever awarded the Nobel Peace Prize for her work.

All machines need grease to run smoothly;
Tammany Hall's machine was just a little greasier than most.

Corrupt *political bosses* pulled the strings of
many government operations at the local, state & national level.
Most notorious of these was *William "Boss" Tweed*
who controlled New York City's *Tammany Hall*
political machine during the 1870's.
Tweed controlled New York's Democratic Party
by providing patronage jobs and assistance
to New York's large Irish immigrant population.
With the support of the voters he helped,
Tweed was able to steer government contracts
toward his cronies, making himself
a multi-millionaire in the process.
Tweed would be brought down by investigative reporters and
by the cartoons of *Thomas Nast* in <u>Harper's Weekly</u>
who revealed the depths of his schemes.
Although Tweed would die in jail,
corruption during the Gilded Age was endemic.

"No; it's '<u>K</u>nights of Labor' with a 'K;'"

"'<u>Nights</u> of Labor' would be even worse than the 12-hour days and 6-day weeks we have now."

"We're not stupid, you know."

American factory workers would struggle for decades
to form labor unions that could combat
the overwhelming advantage enjoyed by management and
improve the horrendous working conditions typical of the era.
72-hour work-weeks for little pay,
with no benefits or pension in spite of working
in incredibly hazardous conditions were common.
The *National Labor Union* formed in 1866 and quickly
expanded to over 600,000 members by recruiting all types of
workers without exception, a remarkably progressive strategy
for such a racist and misogynistic era. Following in its wake
would be the *Knights of Labor* which would surpass the NLU
in membership during the 1880's,
but which would be brought down due to association
with the *Haymarket Square bombing* in Chicago in 1886.
Workers striking at the McCormick Harvester plant
met at the square on May 4th,
but in the midst of their gathering a bomb exploded
that killed seven policemen.
Eight anarchists would be tried with seven sentenced to death
even though the perpetrator was never discovered.
Ultimately, the only major union that would thrive and survive
from this era was the *American Federation of Labor*,
organized by *Samuel Gompers* that only included
skilled tradespeople and focused on salaries &
working conditions rather than on a political agenda.

"No, I keep trying to tell you;
there were three big strikes,
but baseball wasn't even popular yet."

"There was an incipient labor movement that
strove to improve the lives and working conditions
for the masses of unskilled workers
toiling in American factories…"

"Never mind; just read the next page."

"I'm so glad Prohibition is still decades away;
I definitely need a drink."

The *Great Railroad Strike of 1877* paralyzed transportation over 11 states by shutting down $^2/_3$ of the nation's railroads. Over half a million workers left their posts to protest wage cuts. President Rutherford B. Hayes used federal troops to break the strike, leading to over 100 deaths. A cut in wages also led to the *Homestead Strike* of 1892. Andrew Carnegie's associate *Henry Frick* ruthlessly put down a strike after employees of Carnegie Steel's newest plant occupied the factory to protest the 20% cut in their salaries. 16 people would die before the plant was retaken by Frick's forces. The *Pullman Strike* would take place two years later when workers at the Illinois factory that made opulent railroad sleeping cars were forced to take a 33% cut in their wages, with no corresponding cut in the rents or prices in the company town where the workers lived. A sympathy strike from the workers of the *American Railway Union* who refused to operate trains containing any Pullman cars brought the American railroad system to a standstill. President *Grover Cleveland* had the railroads hook US Mail cars to the trains, and then used his power to break the strike as it was impeding the delivery of the mail. ARU president *Eugene Debs* would be imprisoned, and his frustration would lead him to run for the presidency five times as the candidate of the American Socialist Party.

"These businesses are breaking rules faster than I can write them."

With an increasing number of Americans outraged by
the power wielded and often abused by big business,
Congress in 1890 passed the *Sherman Antitrust Act*.
The law prohibited
"every contract, combination,
or conspiracy in restraint of trade,"
& any "monopolization, attempted monopolization,
or conspiracy or combination to monopolize."
The Sherman Antitrust act was vague and applied
only to interstate commerce,
and would be used effectively only a handful of times,
most frequently against organized labor,
an outcome diametrically opposed to the intent of the law.
Only in 1914 with the passage of the *Clayton Antitrust Act*
would federal restraint over monopolistic practices
gain credible power and protect labor unions from prosecution.
The law followed the *Interstate Commerce Act* of 1887
which was the first federal legislation intended to govern trade,
and which created the *Interstate Commerce Commission*,
regarded as the first significant and enduring
federal bureaucracy.

"What are you crying about?"

"Everything looks fine from up here."

The 1880's and 1890's saw the rise of one of the United States' most significant third-party alternatives.
The *Populist Party* provided a voice for farmers and workers who felt that the political establishment was merely a pawn of the wealthy industrialists and the trusts that monopolized American business.
The Populist platform advocated for a *progressive income tax*, the *direct election of senators*, an expansion of the money supply through *unlimited coinage of silver*, *governmental control of utilities*, an *eight-hour workday* and the *initiative & referendum* to expand the people's voice in politics.
The Populist Party would elect several congressmen, senators and governors and would control the legislatures of four states.
James Weaver would even earn 22 electoral votes and over 1,000,000 popular votes in the 1892 presidential election.
Primarily a party of rural America, immigrant workers never truly embraced the party and the reluctance of Southern whites to participate alongside African Americans ultimately prevented the Populist Party from fully asserting its potential for political power.

"Well,
being crucified upon a cross of gold
does sound pretty bad,
but so does being gut-shot by an anarchist,
so maybe it's okay that McKinley beat me in the election."

The most powerful force within the Populist movement
was *William Jennings Bryan*, a Nebraska congressman
who galvanized support for the coinage of silver
at an inflationary 16:1 ratio to gold.
Bryan's famous *"Cross of Gold"* speech would propel him
to national prominence, and the "Great Commoner"
became the youngest American to ever earn an electoral vote
when he ran as the candidate
of both the Populist and the Democratic parties
in the presidential election of 1896.
Bryan would be defeated by *William McKinley*
who was supported by the Republican political establishment
led by *Mark Hanna* and by the *"yellow press"* that was
influenced by Hanna's wealth and by threats that industrialists
would close their factories if Bryan were elected,
costing workers their jobs.
Bryan would run for president again in 1900 & 1908
and would serve as Secretary of State under Woodrow Wilson.
Bryan would last appear on the American stage
fighting for the conviction of Tennessee biology teacher
John T. Scopes for having taught Darwin's theory of evolution.

"We're already forced into the back of the bus;
now you're going to throw us <u>under</u> the bus?"
"Some 'land of the free' this turned out to be!"

In what has come to be widely-regarded as
one of the worst decisions in the history
of the US Supreme Court,
a 7-1 decision in the 1896 case of *Plessy v. Ferguson*
upheld the doctrine of "*separate but equal*"
as far as treatment based upon race.
Homer Plessy of Louisiana had intentionally entered
a "whites-only" car to protest Louisiana's policy of
segregated facilities as being unconstitutional.
The Court upheld the law,
arguing that the 14th Amendment guaranteed equality
but did not forbid distinctions based upon race.
Justice John Marshall Harlan was the lone dissenter,
asserting that the Constitution is color-blind
and recognizes no establishment of classes among citizens.
It would not be until the landmark 1954 ruling in
Brown v. Board of Education that the Supreme Court
would unanimously overturn its earlier precedent.

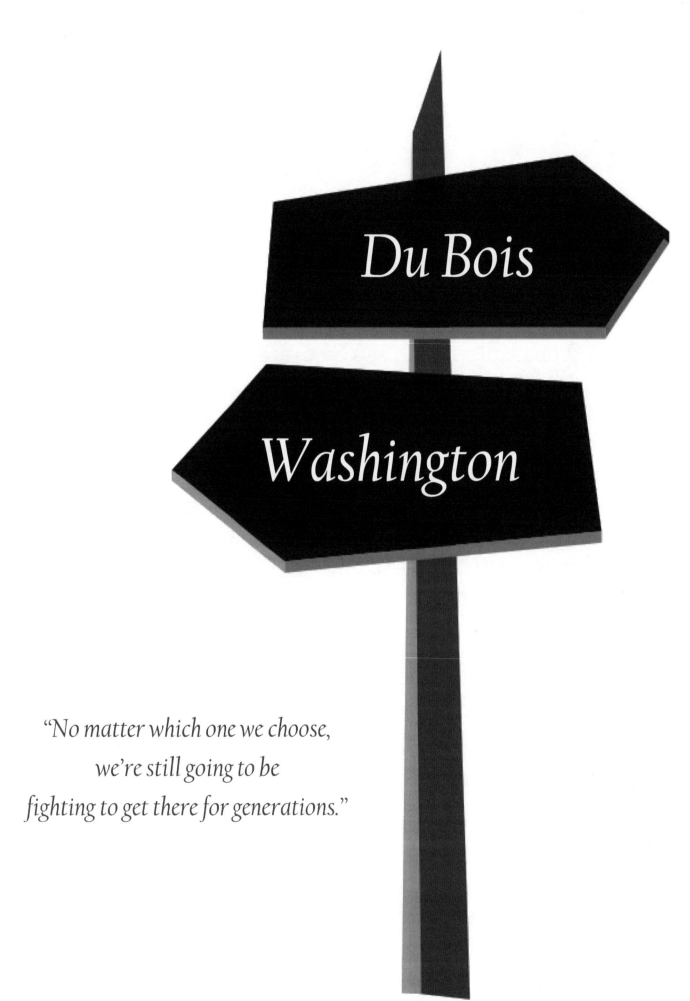

Du Bois

Washington

"No matter which one we choose,
we're still going to be
fighting to get there for generations."

The fight for racial equality would be led
by two dissenting factions as the century came to a close.
Booker T. Washington, a former slave who rose
to become principal of the *Tuskegee Institute*,
favored an *accommodationist* stance regarding racial policy
in which African Americans should aim for job skills which
would foster employment opportunities
while delaying a push for full political equality.
Washington's *"Atlanta Compromise"* was contrasted
by the *Niagara Movement* led by *W.E.B. Du Bois*,
the first African American to earn a doctorate from Harvard.
Du Bois and his allies believed that Washington's strategy
would never compel white Americans to give them equality,
but rather that political access was crucial in order to upend
the racially discriminatory situation in the United States.
Du Bois would be one of the principal founders of the *NAACP*
which remains to this day
the leading force for civil rights in the United States.

"Why did my picture make the book
instead of a cactus or an igloo?"
"All I'm saying is that those expansionists
in the US definitely saved the best for last."

The late 19th century would see the United States
reach its current form. The *Gadsden Purchase* of 1854 would
complete the expansion of the contiguous United States
by acquiring approximately 30,000 square miles
in southern Arizona and southwestern New Mexico
for $10,000,000 to facilitate the construction of a
southern transcontinental railroad route
that would avoid the Rocky Mountains.
Alaska would be purchased from Russia in 1867 for $15,000,000.
Perceived as a foolish waste by many Americans,
"Seward's Folly" ended up providing a wealth of resources
when gold was found in the Yukon and when oil
would be discovered along Alaska's coastline.
Hawaii's acquisition proved the most controversial.
An independent nation ruled by *Queen Liliuokalani*,
the Hawaiian islands had long had an American presence,
first in the form of missionaries, followed by farmers
who established lucrative large-scale sugar plantations.
Hawaii's strategic importance increased as steam began to
power ships and refueling stations were needed
throughout the Pacific.
American businessmen, eager to avoid the high tariff on
foreign sugar levied by the United States, engineered a coup
that overthrew the monarchy in 1893.
The Republic of Hawaii petitioned Congress for its annexation,
but President *Grover Cleveland* refused
given the circumstances of the revolution.
Hawaii would ultimately become a US territory in 1898
when Republican President *William McKinley*
agreed to its annexation. Both Alaska and Hawaii
would formally join the union as states in 1959.

"Everything is fact-checked
and reliable, right?
I'd hate to get my
news from blatantly biased
largely fabricated reporting."

"I mean,
If that's all the
Yellow Press is,
we won't have a reason
to invent
Twitter & Facebook."

While there were many Americans
opposed to foreign adventurism,
most notably the *Anti-Imperialist League* and prominent
figures such as Mark Twain and William Jennings Bryan,
many more Americans were ablaze
with an excessive patriotic enthusiasm
that became known as *"jingoism."*
The lurid *"yellow press"* would print sensationalized stories
that inflamed Americans' appetites for war.
Publishers like *Joseph Pulitzer* of the *New York World*
and *William Randolph Hearst* of the *New York Journal*
would become hugely wealthy and influential by emphasizing
and even fabricating stories to shock and enthrall their readers.

"Do you think
'US NAVY GETS BOMBED IN HAVANA'
has the right ring to it for the headline,
or should we stick with
'REMEMBER THE MAINE'?"

The United States would end a century of *isolationism*
when we would go to war with Spain in 1898.
Cuban rebels had been fighting for independence from Spain
since 1868, and the Spanish had been particularly ruthless
in their efforts to maintain control over the crown jewel
of what remained of the Spanish empire.
American public opinion was stirred up
by tales of Spanish oppression,
and American businesses saw the island
only 90 miles away from Florida
as a golden opportunity to increase profits.
A telegram leaked from the Spanish Ambassador *De Lome*
was highly critical of President McKinley
as a weak leader incapable of standing up for the Cubans.
When 260 American sailors were killed in an explosion
aboard the *USS Maine* docked in Havana harbor
on February 15, 1898,
McKinley asked Congress for a declaration of war.
Following the declaration, Congress would pass
the *Teller Amendment* which pledged that Cuba would be
freed and that the United States had no designs
upon imposing its rule upon the island.

"I don't care which hill it is as long as we take it RIGHT NOW!!!"

*"And where is my *@$!* horse?"*

"We're not called the 'Rough Walkers,' for God's sake!"

The *Spanish-American War* would actually begin
not in Cuba but rather in the Philippines.
Commodore *George Dewey*, on the orders of
Assistant Secretary of the Navy *Theodore Roosevelt*,
had attacked the Spanish fleet in Manila harbor
as soon as news of the war was delivered.
Dewey destroyed Spain's decrepit fleet with no US casualties,
but had to wait months until soldiers arrived to actually
conquer the islands alongside Filipino rebels led by *Emilio
Aguinaldo*. The US would actually spend the next several years
fighting our recent Filipino allies and suffer thousands of
casualties when we refused to abandon control
of the conquered archipelago. The Philippines would ultimately
remain a US territory until 1946. Roosevelt would resign his
position in the Department of the Navy
to lead a volunteer regiment when fighting broke out in Cuba.
The *Battle of San Juan Hill*
(which actually took place at Kettle Hill)
saw Roosevelt lead his *"Rough Riders"* to victory,
even though their horses had not yet arrived
to carry them into battle.
Fewer than 500 US soldiers would lose their lives in combat,
although more than ten times that number died of disease,
and when the US Navy annihilated the Spanish fleet
protecting Cuba, Spain quickly negotiated terms for peace
in what would come to be deemed *"a splendid little war."*

"It's a good thing this is in
black & white,
because you can't tell if this is
the flag of Cuba or Puerto Rico."

"Doesn't matter, though,
because we got them both!
(And the Philippines, and Guam, ...)"

The *Treaty of Paris* that ended the Spanish-American War
found the United States, a nation that had been conceived
in reaction to resentment against ourselves
being a colony of Great Britain, becoming
a colonial power itself.
Cuba would be free, although shackled by the
Platt Amendment which granted the US two military bases on
Cuban soil as well as the right for the US to intervene in Cuba's
affairs at our discretion and which forbade Cuba from
negotiating treaties with other nations of which
the United States did not approve.
The Philippines would remain a US territory
after over 5,000 American and over 200,000 Filipino deaths
suffered during a three-year span of fighting.
Finally, *Puerto Rico* & *Guam* would be sold
to the United States in exchange for $20,000,000 for Spain.
The United States had finally announced its arrival
on the world stage.

"Well if this isn't what John Hay meant by
Open Door policy,
then what in God's name was he talking about?"

The United States quickly began to assert itself
as a force to be reckoned with
as the turn of the century approached.
Dismayed by the *spheres of influence* that had been established
in China by the world's other great imperial powers,
in 1899 Secretary of State *John Hay* proclaimed
an *"Open Door" policy* regarding China in which all nations
would have equal access to trade with China.
The US would join other world powers in suppressing
the *Boxer Rebellion* in China in 1900.
China, however, was given virtually no say in its own affairs,
a reflection of the power-politics and racism
characteristic of the era.

A certain psychoanalyst in Vienna might have some thoughts
regarding this whole "big stick" thing,
but nonetheless President Roosevelt
did get a number of things accomplished.

Upon the assassination of President McKinley in 1901,
McKinley's Vice President *Theodore Roosevelt*
became the youngest man to have ever become president.
Truly one of history's most consequential US presidents,
Roosevelt was a *progressive* egotist
with an almost compulsive need to achieve.
Among his most noteworthy accomplishments were
initiating the construction of the *Panama Canal*,
even though that meant facilitating the independence of Panama
from Colombia; negotiating an end to the *Russo-Japanese War*,
issuing the *Roosevelt Corollary to the Monroe Doctrine*
which cautioned foreign powers out of Latin American affairs
at the expense of a heavy US presence that caused resentment
amongst our neighboring countries; and the sending of the
"Great White Fleet" of 16 US battleships on a world-wide tour.
All of these actions were consistent with Roosevelt's axiom
"speak softly but carry a big stick."
On the domestic front Roosevelt would be known for having
reined-in the power of trusts he felt were abusing
the public interest; preserving vast swaths of the American
wilderness for conservation purposes; and for pursuing his
"Square Deal" for the American people in which he stood
with labor unions fighting onerous working conditions,
and for supporting greater enforcement power for the ICC
to end railroad abuses and supporting the passage
of the *Pure Food & Drug Act* & the *Meat Inspection Act*
that allowed the federal government to inspect consumer items
in an effort to ensure the safety
of what American families were purchasing.

"Well,
you know how we call them
'hot dogs?'"

"They're certainly hot,
that's for sure;"

"And that second part?"

"Let's just say it's a good idea
to keep your dog on a leash."

A significant impetus behind the *Progressive* movement
of the early 20th century was the work of a group
of investigative journalists known as *"muckrakers."*
Authors and reporters strove to shine a light on the injustices
of life in the US, in the hopes of notoriety leading
to a public demand for change and government regulation.
Ida Tarbell in her 1902 book
The History of the Standard Oil Company
exposed that company's unfair practices which would lead
to its monopoly being broken up by the government.
Photojournalist *Jacob Riis* published
How the Other Half Lives in 1890,
opening the eyes of the upper classes
to the poverty of the urban poor, while *Lincoln Steffens*
delineated the political corruption in these same
urban environments in *The Shame of the Cities* in 1904.
Most notably, *Upton Sinclair's The Jungle*,
which he had written with the intent of describing the horrible
working conditions in Chicago's meat-packing plants,
ended up disgusting the entire nation with his descriptions
of the dangerous and gross food products
that were being stocked on America's shelves.

"59 seconds?"

"But I just ordered a drink from the stewardess."

"And how am I supposed to finish this movie?"

On December 17th, 1903
progress of another type was made
in *Kitty Hawk*, North Carolina.
Bicycle mechanics *Wilbur & Orville Wright* of Dayton Ohio
successfully flew the first powered airplane,
covering 852 feet in 59 seconds.
Powered flight would improve quickly and steadily,
and in barely a single generation, airplanes would be able to fly
coast-to-coast and even across the Atlantic Ocean.
Thanks to the Wright Brothers,
the United States can justly claim to have soared
higher, faster and farther than any other nation.

"You can have any color you want,
as long as it's black."

"I'm talking about the cars, not the workers."

In 1908, *Henry Ford* debuted the *Model T* and revolutionized the American automotive industry. The Model T was priced at $825 and provided basic, reliable transportation via an ***internal combustion engine*** that soon replaced earlier technologies for automobiles that included electric and steam-powered engines. Ford did not invent the car, but his application of *Frederick W. Taylor's* principles of ***scientific management*** and efficiency allowed Ford to perfect the manufacturing of cars via the ***assembly line***. Skilled craftsmen who had built cars from beginning to end could now be replaced by workers who only performed one repetitive task. Ford doubled the average daily wage to $5 to induce workers to stay through what was often mind-numbing work and so as to facilitate a base of customers who could afford to purchase his vehicles. The price of a Model T would drop to $290 by the end of its production run, and over 15,000,000 would be sold, a number that wouldn't be equaled until 1972 by the Volkswagen Beetle.

Ford and his fellow automakers centered in Detroit, Michigan made the US a car-loving country and made auto manufacturing the nation's biggest industry. Ford would become incredibly wealthy, but his personal hostility toward Jews, immigrants, and African Americans has tainted his reputation from a modern perspective.

"I won the Nobel Peace Prize!"

"How could I lose to a socialist ex-con,
a nerdy professor,
and a guy so fat they needed to install
a new bathtub in the White House?"

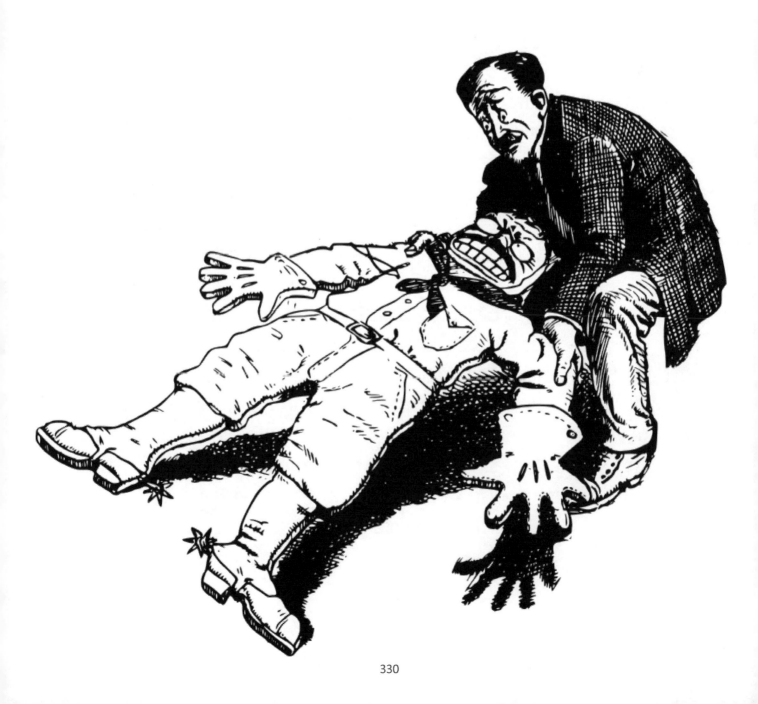

While Theodore Roosevelt is justifiably celebrated
for the impact he had upon US history,
his political career would ultimately end on a sour note.
Having pledged to serve only two terms as president,
Roosevelt left the White House with *William Howard Taft*
elected in 1908 as his Republican successor.
Taft was less progressive than Roosevelt had expected,
and when Taft supported the *Payne-Aldrich Tariff* which
raised rates on imports and fired Roosevelt's conservationist
ally *Gifford Pinchot*, Roosevelt began to bitterly criticize
his loyal former Secretary of War. By 1912 Roosevelt's ego led
him to seek re-nomination as the Republican candidate
for president. When Taft kept the nomination,
Roosevelt ran as the nominee of a new party,
the *Progressive (Bull Moose) Party*. Roosevelt would outpoll
Taft in the popular vote, but with the two Republicans splitting
their party's votes and Socialist candidate *Eugene Debs* earning
5% of the popular vote, Democrat *Woodrow Wilson*
became the first Democrat
elected to the White House since 1892.

"No doubt this will install total confidence in our elections forever and ever."

"Thank God we'll never have anyone call into question the legitimacy of our electoral process."

The Progressive Era presidencies of Roosevelt, Taft & Wilson
would see the inception of a number of reforms.
The *Australian (secret) ballot* would help negate the power of
political bosses to steer elections in their favor;
direct primaries would allow the people to determine who the
candidates for office would be rather than party elites;
the *16th Amendment* would allow for a *progressive income
tax* on the wealthiest Americans earning over $3000/year,
while the *17th Amendment* would allow for a state's citizens
to *directly elect their US senators* rather than state
legislatures doing so as the Constitution
had originally established.
Finally, on the state and local levels,
the initiative, referendum & recall were introduced.
The *initiative* allowed a petition by voters
to compel legislatures to vote on an issue;
The *referendum* allowed for petitioners to demand
that a popular vote be taken on a given issue; &
the *recall* allowed a sufficient number of voters to compel
an elected official to stand for a vote of confidence
prior to the end of their term due to
a lack of satisfaction with their performance.

"I had a sinking feeling
that this was going to happen."

"Too soon?"

When the 1914 assassination of Archduke Franz Ferdinand of Austro-Hungary plunged much of Europe into *World War I,* President Wilson championed the neutrality of the United States. He would even run his 1916 presidential re-election campaign on the slogan that *"he kept us out of war."* Both the British declaration of a naval blockade around Germany and German U-boats attacking allied shipping posed grave threats to American efforts to maintain the freedom of the seas. Wilson's policy would first be put to the test when 128 Americans aboard the *Lusitania* were drowned when the British passenger vessel was torpedoed by the Germans. Unbeknownst to the public was that the Lusitania was carrying several million rounds of ammunition for the Allies, making it a legitimate target for the Germans, although the Germans could not have known that. Wilson would protest the sinking, and when additional American lives were lost aboard the *Arabic* & the *Sussex*, Germany issued the *Sussex Pledge* in which they promised not to sink merchant or passenger ships without warning.

*"We would have offered Florida too,
but we knew nobody would have wanted it."*

March 1st, 1917 saw the publication of a decrypted telegram
sent from German foreign minister Arthur *Zimmermann*
to the Mexican government that offered
Texas, New Mexico & Arizona back to Mexico
in exchange for Mexico coming into the war
against the Allies as a distraction to the United States.
Americans were widely roused by this clandestine offer,
and President Wilson saw clearly
that open conflict with Germany was likely unavoidable.

"Sometimes history needs a push."
(That's a real quote from Lenin;
sometimes this side of the book can be educational too!)

Wilson's resolve was further strengthened
when the *Russian Revolution*
overthrew the Czar on March 15th, 1917.
Previous misgivings about joining an alliance
with the autocratic Russian empire were swept aside,
and when five additional unarmed US merchant ships
fell prey to U-boat attacks,
Wilson asked for and received a declaration of war
"to make the world safe for democracy."

"It has been a horrible four years,
but since it's the 'War to end All Wars,'
we won't ever have to deal with the likes of this again."
"And certainly not in another 21 years; don't be absurd."

The armies of both the *Allies* and the *Central Powers*
had been mired in *trench warfare* along the *Western Front*
between France & Germany for most of the war.
The *American Expeditionary Force*
led by *General John Pershing*
initially plugged holes in the Allied lines,
but by the summer of 1918, American troops
would fight independently at battles such as
Belleau Wood and the *Battle of the Marne*.
Both sides were exhausted,
and it was more the threat of fresh and well-equipped
reinforcements from the United States
than actual American successes on the battlefield
that would ultimately convince the Central Powers
to surrender on *November 11th, 1918*.

"Wilson has 14 Points?"
"The good lord only had 10!"
"Let's just work this out amongst ourselves, okay?"

With the Great War ended, President Wilson traveled to France to negotiate *"peace without victory."*
Basking in adulation and overconfident in himself, Wilson pursued an agenda he called his *14 Points*.
Wilson's idealistic goals included arms reduction, freedom of navigation, self-determination for ethnic groups, an end to secret treaties and, most important, a *League of Nations* where diplomacy and negotiation would replace war. The other Allied leaders were more jaded and vengeful against the defeated Central Powers and eroded Wilson's agenda, but the president stood firm on *Article X* which created the League.
Wilson had imprudently snubbed Republican involvement in his peace delegation, and when he returned home had to face isolationists in the Senate led by Senator *Henry Cabot Lodge*.
A group of senators known as *"Irreconcilables"* opposed the treaty altogether, while Lodge's *"Reservationist"* faction mandated a weakened League. Wilson tried to work around Republican opposition by traveling the United States on a speaking tour, but his arduous efforts led to him suffering a debilitating stroke that would incapacitate him for the duration of his presidency. The Senate would defeat the treaty Wilson envisioned and, when proposed with reservations, the Democrats joined the Irreconcilables to defeat it again.
Wilson's vision of a world united for peace would be dashed, as the US negotiated a separate peace treaty with Germany and never joined the League of Nations. A shattered Wilson would remain secluded in the White House for the remainder of his term, with many speculating that his wife Edith and a coterie of close assistants were fulfilling his duties until Republican *Warren G. Harding* replaced Wilson as President.

"You can't just yell 'movie'
in a crowded firehouse."

"Wait a second;
I may have screwed that up."

The expansion of federal authority during the war included several restrictions on personal liberties. The *Espionage Act* made it illegal to encourage resistance within the military or to obstruct the *Selective Service Act* which drafted 4,800,000 into the armed forces. The *Sedition Act* made it illegal to criticize the government or to utter "disloyal" statements. Over 1,000 people would be convicted and jailed during the war, including Socialist leader *Eugene Debs* who would be sentenced to 10 years for speaking out against the war effort. Debs would run for president from jail in 1920, garnering approximately a million votes.

In 1919, the US Supreme Court would rule in *Schenk v. United States* that the Espionage & Sedition Acts were constitutional, deciding that Schenk's efforts to distribute pamphlets opposing the war presented *"a clear and present danger"* to national security and that he was therefore not protected under the 1st Amendment.

"Well Mildred,
I hope you're satisfied;"
You and these other hellions
can finally vote."

"But only after you
clean the house,
cook my meals,
look after the children, ..."

1920 would see a great and long-overdue step toward equality when the *19th Amendment* would be ratified guaranteeing women the right to vote in all elections. Although several states, primarily in the west, had already allowed women to vote, *suffragettes* had battled for generations to guarantee the franchise to all women. Leaders such as *Carrie Chapman Catt* of the *National American Woman Suffrage Association* and *Alice Paul* of the *National Woman's Party* marched, agitated, and endured arrests & hunger strikes to generate support for the enfranchisement of women. It would finally be the support for the war effort embraced by these women that would turn the tide of opposition and enable half of the adult population to finally have their voice heard in affairs of state.

"Well honey;
remember how you always said
'I'm dying to get the right to vote?'"
"It's funny how things have worked out..."

Just as the world finally drew a collective sigh of relief with the
end of the Great War in 1918, a global flu pandemic gripped the
US in its clutches. Beginning in a US Army boot camp in Kansas,
soldiers headed to Europe carried the virus that would come to
be known as the *Spanish Flu*. With no effective treatments
or vaccines, an estimated 50,000,000 people would die
worldwide, with over 600,000 Americans included.
By the time the pandemic had run its course in 1921,
the flu would infect over 500,000,000 people
and result in more fatalities than the recent war.

*Likely not the drinking problem
that the temperance movement was decrying,
but vexing nevertheless…*

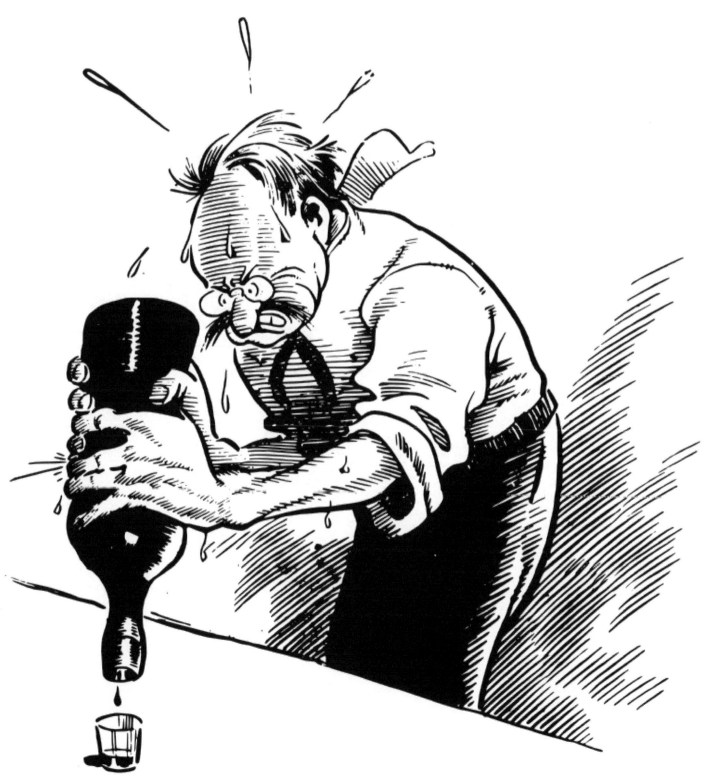

The *18th Amendment* would be ratified in 1919,
authorizing Congress to pass the *Volstead Act*
which forbade the manufacture, transportation
and sale of alcohol.
The *Prohibition* era would last until 1933,
and stand out as an abject failure of trying to legislate morality.
The 18th Amendment is unique because it is the only
amendment to the Constitution that both restricted
individual freedoms and because it is the only amendment
that has ever been repealed.
In spite of the harm that the consumption of alcohol had
clearly caused to American society, widespread flouting of the
restrictions throughout the nation led to the flourishing
of *organized crime* syndicates such as the *Mafia*,
which found a market ripe for exploitation.
As the 1920's wore on, gangsters such as *Al Capone*
would generate more revenue than the federal government,
and when Prohibition ended, these criminal enterprises
had firmly established themselves on the American landscape.
There were exceptions to the restrictions on alcohol
such as consumption for religious or medicinal purposes,
but smuggling, stockpiling and moonshining
became everyday occurrences for many Americans.

"We'll go after the unions first,
then we'll go after the Socialists,
try to find some anarchists to rough up,
and then there's some baseball team in Cincinnati
that we'd better look into …"

No sooner had the United States ended its brief involvement
in World War I than a new threat appeared,
much closer on the horizon. The *Red Scare* would find its roots
in the nativism and *xenophobia* that had characterized much of
American history. Following dozens of bombs being sent in
packages through the mail in 1919, Attorney General
A. Mitchell Palmer cracked down on anarchists, socialists
and communists in the United States.
Paranoia confirmed by the communist revolution in Russia
made many Americans fearful of a similar uprising
in the United States and, as a consequence, Palmer
commissioned a young *J. Edgar Hoover* to begin investigating,
arresting and prosecuting many immigrants and citizens
suspected of holding "un-American" viewpoints. Hoover would
go on to create and lead the *FBI* until his death in 1972,
investigating dissidents, criminals and everyday Americans
suspected of threatening behaviors or ideologies.
Palmer and Hoover would arrest over 6,000 people,
with over 500 being deported. Palmer's influence would wane
after his predictions of widespread riots
on May 1st, 1920 failed to come to fruition,
but the fear of communism would remain and would
reappear as a *2nd Red Scare* during the 1940's and 1950's.

I'm sure it will come as quite a shock
to all of you reading this in the 21st century,
but not all Americans
were of a like mind regarding immigration.

While the plaque on the Statue of Liberty may read
"give me your tired, your poor, your huddled masses
yearning to breathe free,"
in practice, the United States would be anything but welcoming
during the 1920's. The *Immigration Act of 1917* had forbidden
any immigrants from the Middle East to southeast Asia.
The *Emergency Quota Act* of 1921 would cap immigration at
357,000 people/year and would restrict the number of
immigrants from a given country to 3% of the number of
immigrants from that same country who had already been in the
United States in 1910. The *National Origins Act of 1924* would
tighten restrictions further, with the percentage reduced to 2%
of those who had immigrated in 1890. These restrictions were
intentionally established to reduce the numbers of southern
and eastern European immigrants in favor of immigrants from
northern & western Europe. Prejudice against Catholics, Jews
and Eastern Orthodox Christians lay at the root of
these policies. By 1927, Japanese immigrants joined the Chinese
immigrants who had been banned altogether in the
Chinese Exclusion Act of 1882 and the immigration quota
was lowered to 150,000/year.
Exceptions were made for immigrants from
Canada and Mexico, who were allowed to immigrate
to meet the need for labor in the western United States.

"What we lack in intellect, compassion & civility we make up for in savagery, inbreeding & stupid outfits."

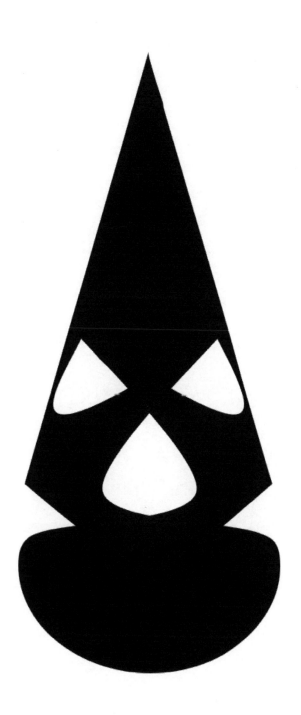

An ugly reactionary impulse took hold in many parts of America during the 1920's, manifested most notably in the flourishing of a resurgent *Ku Klux Klan*. Opposing not only African Americans during this era, the Klan would grow to over 5,000,000 members who publicly denounced Catholics, Jews, union members & immigrants as well. Even governors and members of Congress openly touted their membership, and the Klan reached well beyond the South into the Midwest and the Plains. The outrageous and horrific terrorism of the Klan and its ilk were most grievously demonstrated in 1921 when the *Greenwood* neighborhood of *Tulsa, Oklahoma* was destroyed, causing millions of dollars in damage and leaving 10,000 African-Americans homeless after their thriving community was attacked in an act of racial hatred. Several hundred would die and scores more be hurt for having tried to defend a young Black man who had allegedly assaulted a White teenager, a charge for which he was later exonerated. The *Great Migration* of African Americans from the South to large northern cities that had started during the war years would accelerate as the violence of white supremacists became more and more pronounced. The Klan's public acceptability would be damaged by an embezzlement scandal and by the murder conviction of Indiana's Grand Dragon, the leader of the Klan who killed another Klansman in 1925. Unfortunately, the Klan and the hatred it espouses endure to the present day.

"It says here that Bryan was a great intellect;
I wonder why he holds onto such a backward belief?"

"He's really going to flip his lid
When <u>Planet of the Apes</u> comes out!"

There was no greater symbol of the clash between the modern sensibilities of the *"Roaring 20's"* and the *fundamentalism* of mainstream conservatism than the *Scopes Monkey Trial* of 1925. Tennessee biology teacher *John Scopes* was approached by the *ACLU* to violate a state law that prohibited the teaching of *Darwin's theory of evolution*. Championing the prosecution's case was the "Great Orator" *William Jennings Bryan*, while *Clarence Darrow* led Scopes' defense. Scopes had clearly broken the law and would be convicted, but the public coverage of the trial on the now widely-popular *radio* networks that brought news of the dramatic case across the nation made the rural creationists look foolish & backwards, and Bryan would die five days later, crushed by his humiliation. Scopes would be fined $100, and Tennessee would not repeal its law mandating the teaching of creationism in its public schools until 1967.

"Dolores, I've never found myself more attracted to a woman,
but since there are no condoms legally available,
I shall content myself with looking longingly at you from a distance."

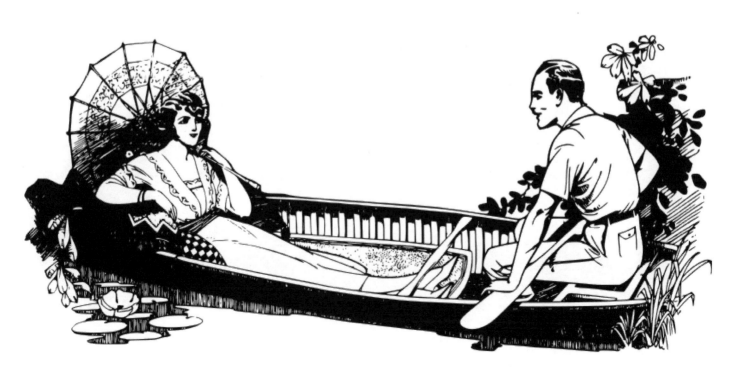

Reflecting the more liberal viewpoints of the modern age, *Margaret Sanger* would help to advance the cause of women throughout much of the 20th century. Sanger's mother had died at age 49 after having 18 pregnancies in 22 years, and Sanger would make it her life's work to make birth control available to American women. Sanger would be prosecuted in 1914 for having published <u>Family Limitation</u> which violated the *Comstock Act* for its sexual content. Sanger fled to Great Britain, but when she returned she opened the nation's first birth control clinic in 1916, where she would again be arrested for having given a family planning pamphlet to an undercover policewoman. Sanger was an opponent of abortion in most cases, and simply wanted women to be able to control whether they chose to become pregnant or not. Fighting for the right of married women to be prescribed access to condoms which were then illegal would help to prevent back-alley abortions that were taking the lives of many women who found themselves with no alternative for an unplanned pregnancy. Sanger would found the **American Birth Control League** in 1921, which would evolve eventually into Planned Parenthood of America. Sanger's efforts, as well as a liberalization of divorce laws which made it easier for women to escape from unhappy marriages would be a significant step toward greater equality for women in the United States.

"Better drink up;
the 30's are going to be another story entirely."

When *Warren Harding* campaigned for the presidency in 1920, he pledged to achieve a *"return to normalcy."* For better and for worse, that is what the three Republican presidents accomplished. The 1920's reflected a cynicism and disenchantment with the rest of the world that resulted from the failure of American efforts to achieve a peace without victory in World War I. Harding's tenure would be tarnished by the *Teapot Dome* scandal, in which his Secretary of the Interior *Albert Fall* sold drilling rights to oil fields in Oklahoma and California to speculators for $385,000. Fall would be the first cabinet secretary ever imprisoned for the scandal, and Attorney General *Harry Daugherty* would be fired for having looked the other way. Harding's term was cut short when he died of a heart attack in 1923, to be succeeded by *Calvin Coolidge*. "Quiet Cal" would continue the Republican agenda of low taxes on the wealthy and high tariffs. *Herbert Hoover* would round out the Republican triumvirate of presidents and would promise Americans "a car in every garage and a chicken in every pot." While many farmers suffered due to falling prices caused by overproduction during the 1920's, most Americans got caught up in an explosion of consumer spending motivated by advertising and the availability of easy *credit*. Everyday Americans were fueled by their confidence in the stock market which, thanks to *margin-buying,* allowed even middle-class Americans to aspire to great wealth, thanks to investments in companies which seemed to be continually headed for greater and greater profits.

"I can't tell from this distance,
but I'd wager that none of those people rushing to form a dove of peace
are Nazis from Germany or Fascists from Italy or militarists from Japan."

"They're all busy rushing somewhere else to build up modern militaries
that are going to kick the crap right out of these pacifist ideologues."

While the experience of World War I had led many Americans to retreat toward our isolationist heritage, there were several significant international engagements by the United States during the 1920's. The *Five-Power Treaty* of 1921 established a limit on the relative sizes of the naval fleets of Great Britain, the US, Japan, Italy & France. The *Nine-Power Treaty* confirmed respect for the sovereignty of long-suffering China. The *Kellogg-Briand Pact* of 1928 would lead to 64 nations renouncing offensive war, although the lack of any enforcement mechanism and the allowance of defensive wars made the agreement essentially meaningless. Finally, the *Dawes Act* of 1924 created a cumbersome structure by which the US lent money to Germany in order to enable Germany to pay $30,000,000,000 in *reparations* to Great Britain & France so that they could repay the United States the $10,000,000,000 that had been lent to the Allies during the war. The payment structure helped in keeping the international economy afloat, but when the Great Depression arrived the agreement would collapse and the world would descend into economic chaos.

"Things were still so racist in the 20's that I'm surprised they didn't put this page in the back of the book."

The 1920's couldn't be considered the *Jazz Age*
without the contributions of African Americans
who flourished in the urban centers of the North
such as Chicago, Detroit and, most notably, New York.
By the 1920's, almost 200,000 African Americans would call
Harlem their home, and a center of Black culture and art would
blossom forth in what is now known as
the *Harlem Renaissance.*
Langston Hughes, Duke Ellington,
Bessie Smith & Louis Armstrong
are only a few of the performers who became
successful and influential, despite the fact that they
weren't allowed to dine or stay in the locations
where they performed due to the rigid segregation
policies that existed even in the North.

"I am so committed to an all-black experience that I insisted that I only be represented in silhouette."

Marcus Garvey was a Jamaican immigrant to the United States who embraced the strategy of W.E.B. DuBois but went a step further and advocated for *black separatism* and even a return to Africa.
Garvey operated a number of prominent businesses including the <u>Negro World</u> newspaper and the *Black Star Line* shipping company.
Garvey believed so strongly in separate communities with separate schools, businesses and institutions for African Americans that he collaborated with the Ku Klux Klan due to the similarity of their goals.
Garvey envisioned the Black Star Line helping to transit African Americans back to Africa to settle in Liberia.
Garvey would be convicted of mail fraud for stock swindles regarding his companies and would be jailed for two years, after which he was deported to Jamaica.
Garvey's Black nationalism was tainted by his association with the Klan and by his outspoken prejudice against Jews and people of mixed race.

In 1977, the Governor of Massachusetts
declared Sacco & Vanzetti innocent.
Maybe they were right to be hostile to government after all.

The pervasiveness of prejudice and xenophobia was nowhere more evident than in the trial of Italian immigrants Nicola Sacco & Bartolomeo Vanzetti in 1921. Convicted of a murder that took place in Massachusetts while the payroll of a shoe factory was being stolen, the trial of *Sacco & Vanzetti* drew international attention. An outwardly prejudiced judge condemned them to death, even though ballistics evidence was inconclusive and after another criminal confessed to the crime. Anti-immigrant hostility and Sacco & Vanzetti's belief in *anarchy* were the true culprits in their 1927 execution.

*"I'm delighted that everyone is so impressed,
but the truth is that I had a bunch of frequent-flyer miles
that were about to expire,
and I just didn't want them to go to waste."*

In May of 1927, *Charles Lindbergh* astonished the world
as he became the first pilot to fly solo across the Atlantic,
covering 3,600 miles in a 33 $\frac{1}{2}$ –hour flight
from New York to Paris. Lindbergh's flight in
the *Spirit of St. Louis* made him <u>Time</u> magazine's first
"Man of the Year" and brought him great wealth and celebrity.
His elation would be dashed five years later when his infant son
was kidnapped and murdered, riveting the nation
in what has been called "the crime of the century."
The crime would lead to Congress declaring kidnapping a
federal crime, and the hysteria regarding the tragedy would lead
Lindbergh and his family to emigrate to Europe.
Lindbergh would later become somewhat nefarious for his
isolationist political stance, his regard for the Nazi regime,
and for his support for the anti-war *America First Committee*.

*"Perhaps coffins might be a sound investment
over the next several years?"*

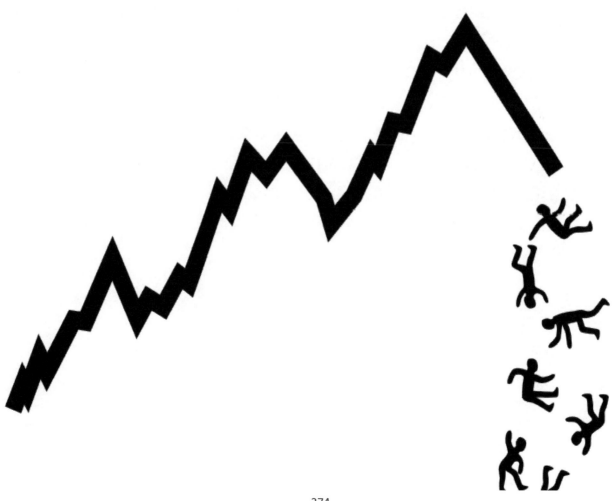

While Lindbergh was flying to new heights,
the US stock market was rivaling his ascent.
The *Dow Jones Industrial Average* reflected the confidence and
enthusiasm of the American consumer, and over the span of
18 months doubled in value. The boom was fueled by credit and
speculation, and as supply exceeded the demand for goods and
services that were being produced, a crash inevitably followed.
Black Thursday (October 24, 1929) saw a precipitous drop
in the market. Bankers and financiers bought millions of shares
hoping to prop up prices, but on October 29th, *Black Tuesday*,
the bottom fell out. Panic-selling and *margin-calls* reduced the
market to a shambles, and by the end of Hoover's term in 1932,
the Dow would drop from its pre-crash high of 381 to 41,
eviscerating the savings of millions of Americans and helping
to plunge the United States into the *Great Depression*.

"I know; let's try cutting ourselves off from our biggest market to increase sales; we haven't tried that yet; what's the worst thing that could happen?"

Just in case the *Great Depression* might have been avoided,
President Herbert Hoover decided to give the economy just the
push it needed to precipitate a global financial meltdown.
In June of 1930, President Hoover signed the
Hawley-Smoot Tariff into law. The tariff raised rates
to the highest level in US history. Hoover's motivation
was to protect American corporate profits,
but the outcome was catastrophic. Foreign nation
unsurprisingly retaliated with tariff increases of their own,
and America's foreign sales dried up almost instantly.
Further, American consumers faced higher prices
thanks to the lack of foreign competition.

As most any American would have attested,
the vacuum wasn't the only Hoover that sucked.

President Hoover believed in the Republican creed of small government. Hoover feared that federal relief for suffering Americans would lead to a weak spirit and a rejection of the *Puritan work ethic* that had made America great. Hoover insisted that

"although the people support the government, the government should not support the people."

As the economy continued to collapse with
25% of Americans out of work;
with GDP being cut in half;
with the money supply contracting by $\frac{1}{3}$;
with the savings of 10,000,000 Americans
wiped out following the collapse of 20% of American banks;
and with the creation of ramshackle slums dubbed
"Hoovervilles" housing thousands of America's most destitute, Hoover finally decided to take action.

Hoover supported the creation of the *Reconstruction Finance Corporation* to provide financial subsidies for large businesses in the hope of propping them up so as to maintain employment. Hoover's focus on the *trickle-down* benefits of *supply-side economic theory* would prove woefully inadequate to the task, and by the time World War I veterans arrived in Washington DC as part of the *Bonus Army* to demand promised benefits early, Hoover responded by calling in the military who killed two veterans while clearing out the protestors with tanks and tear gas.

"Truth be told, I wasn't planning on doing the broadcast from here,
but the wheel on my wheelchair had a flat tire
and I was stuck here by the fire."

"Talk about a happy accident;
'Desk-side chat' doesn't quite have the same ring to it."

Democrat *Franklin Delano Roosevelt* would win
the presidential election of 1932 and would go on to become the
only president ever elected more than twice,
winning re-election in 1936, 1940 & 1944.
Although coming from a background of wealth and privilege,
FDR was a charismatic speaker who connected effectively with
his fellow Americans. Left disabled by a 1921 bout with polio,
Roosevelt was able to empathize with the suffering of others,
and he would demonstrate his fidelity to his countrymen
by using the radio to connect with and support the people
of the United States through a series of broadcasts that became
known as *"fireside chats."* Roosevelt's compassion, intellect
and willingness to try a wide variety of approaches in dealing
with the causes and consequences of the financial crisis,
as well as his leadership during the dark days of World War II,
would cement his reputation as one of
America's greatest leaders. Roosevelt's admonition that
"the only thing we have to fear is fear itself"
provided the *"greatest generation"* with the courage
and confidence to struggle through tremendous adversity.

Okay; the New Deal wasn't <u>this</u> good,

but definitely at least a full house, which is nothing to sneeze at.

Roosevelt's strategy for dealing with the problems
of the Great Depression came to be known as the *New Deal*.
Working with a team of intellectuals and academics who
became known as the ***Brain Trust***, Roosevelt would implement
a host of federal initiatives with varying degrees of success.
The reach and power of the federal government would expand
to an extent unprecedented in US history,
much to the chagrin of conservative Republicans.
Roosevelt's famous ***"first 100 days"*** in office
would see the passage of more significant legislation
than during any equivalent period in US history.
Part of FDR's brilliance was knowing when to try a new
approach and his willingness to acknowledge that a program
wasn't succeeding. Roosevelt's New Deal would ultimately
prove so successful, that despite the conservative
Supreme Court ruling several of his new federal programs
unconstitutional, FDR would be re-elected in 1936 with even
greater Democratic majorities in Congress and would go on
to institute a ***2nd New Deal*** during the ensuing four years.

As Mrs. Keynes would tell you,
John Maynard knew a whole lot
about stimulating demand.

And everybody knows that
the ladies can't resist a man
with an Economics degree.

Roosevelt's plan for stimulating economic growth
rejected the trickle-down economics of the 1920's
in favor of Keynesian economic principles.
British economist *John Maynard Keynes* believed
that during periods of economic stress,
governments needed to spend more to
"prime the pump" of the nation's economy,
even if that meant running a deficit.
Keynes' theory was that government spending
that put money into the hands of the people would lead to
a resurgence of spending that would revitalize the economy,
and that taxes would ultimately address the government debt
that accrued as the economy was being stimulated.

"I don't care if it's the Three "R's,"
the Three Little Pigs,
or Three Blind Mice,
but if I can't scrape up three square meals a day,
it's going to be three strikes and I'm out."

Roosevelt felt that the battle for the economic health of the nation had to be waged on three fronts. The New Deal would focus on *relief, recovery & reform*. *Relief* referenced providing direct assistance to the poor and suffering so that families could have food on the table and a roof over their heads. *Recovery* focused on getting America's businesses and institutions stabilized and operational so that they could employ American workers and build the nation's GDP back up to where it had been. *Reform* programs were designed to ensure that the factors that had led the nation to its precarious position would not plunge the United States into another depression when business cycles took a downturn in future generations.

If you're banking on a funny joke here,
you're likely to be disappointed.
(groan implied)

In order to restore confidence in America's banking system,
Roosevelt ordered a *bank holiday* on March 6th, 1933.
Banks that reopened after having their books examined
by government auditors made Americans feel secure
about leaving their deposits in the banks,
preventing *bank runs* and subsequent additional bank failures.
The *Emergency Banking Act* allowed solvent bank
to reopen on March 13th. Roosevelt would support the creation
of the *Federal Deposit Insurance Corporation*,
which guaranteed bank deposits up to $2,500,
and which remains in place to this day
with deposits guaranteed up to $250,000.

"No, as a matter of fact I never have heard the story
of the fox guarding the henhouse."

"Don't fret, Sammy; I'll be sure
to look out for the interests of everyone equally."

The stock market too would come to be addressed
by the reforms of the New Deal.
The *Securities and Exchange Commission* would be created to
regulate and monitor the stock market
to ensure that practices were legitimate and responsible.
Joseph P. Kennedy, father of the future president
and himself a self-made millionaire
who had manipulated the market to his own advantage for years
would serve as the first chairman of the SEC.

"Just watch who you're calling an 'unfit chicken,' buster;"

"I will unleash a Kentucky Fried world of hurt on you!"

The *National Recovery Administration* was created in 1933
to facilitate stable profits for businesses and
better working conditions for laborers. The program
temporarily suspended antitrust laws so that industries and
their workers could negotiate reasonable profits and
improved wages and hours for workers.
Participation was voluntary and the program would help
to ameliorate the worst conditions of the financial crisis,
but in 1935 the Supreme Court would unanimously declare
the NRA unconstitutional in *Schechter v. U.S.*
when the court ruled that the NRA violated both separation of
powers between the executive and legislative branches
and the *Commerce Clause* of the Constitution
when it tried to forbid the sales of unfit chickens
by a local butcher.

"It sure is a good thing
that I had a chance
to come out West;
I would never have had a chance
to learn how to use a shovel
back at home."

"And that pickaxe?
I may not be ready for that yet.
Soooo complex and confusing!"

Several million young men found employment
with the *Civilian Conservation Corps*,
a program that took teenagers out of the job market
who might have competed for employment with their fathers
and took them out west to learn skills and work outdoors
on reforestation, flood control, fire prevention
and other environmental projects.
The wages paid to the workers would be sent to their families
while the workers gained experience and had their
room and board paid for by the government,
reducing their families' expenses at home in the process.

The *Public Works Administration* led by
Secretary of the Interior *Harry Hopkins* put millions to work
by providing state and local governments with money to hire
workers constructing roads, bridges, public buildings and dams.
When the PWA would be declared unconstitutional,
it would be replaced by the *Works Progress Administration*
which not only financed construction projects but also
public art and theater and oral histories of everyday Americans.

*"Well, it's certainly lovely to finally have a house
and I don't want to seem ungrateful,
but in truth I had actually been hoping for something a bit bigger."*

The *Federal Housing Administration*
provided government-guaranteed mortgages
to spur the construction industry and to help
poor and middle-class Americans build, buy and repair houses.
While this would help many citizens to achieve this cornerstone
of the American dream, virtually all FHA loans went strictly
to Whites. Furthermore, communities were divided by
"redlining" that allowed investments in some neighborhoods
while restricting loans in others, leading to a distinct separation
between thriving communities and slums.

The *Agricultural Adjustment Administration*
strove to improve the lives of America's farmers
by paying them not to produce.
Paradoxically, as farmers had tried to earn more money
by bringing more of their crops and animals to market,
the abundance of supply had driven down prices
leaving them worse off than before.
Millions of acres of crops were plowed under
and countless animals slaughtered,
and while farm revenue did increase,
the AAA would be another one of the New Deal programs
that would be struck down by the Supreme Court.
The *Resettlement Administration* would subsidize
small farmers with loans and help migrant workers
to relocate to where jobs might more likely be available.
Both programs sought to address the hardships experienced
by America's rural poor.

This is actually a color photograph;
they're just totally covered in dirt stirred up out on the Plains.

Okay; that's not true, but it made for a really compelling caption, didn't it?

Not only America's farmers but the entire nation was plagued
throughout the 1930's by the *Dust Bowl*.
Overgrazing and the plowing up of prairie grasses for farms
had stripped the Plains of millions of tons of topsoil.
Regions that customarily expected as little as 10 inches of rain
annually found themselves unbelievably experiencing even more
arid conditions. 100,000,000 acres lost all pretense of viability as
farmland, with swirling dust storms reducing visibility to only
the length of a person's arm and blocking out the sun as far away
as New York City. The CCC would plant 200,000,000 trees
in an effort to prevent additional erosion
and the Resettlement Administration would attempt to help
3,500,000 *"Okies"* and *"Arkies"* find places
where they could continue to live off the land.

"We're bringing electricity to millions of Americans who still don't have access to it."

"Shocking."

One of the most ambitious undertakings of the New Deal
was the *Tennessee Valley Authority*.
Setting out to completely change one of America's
poorest regions, the TVA was a series of 17 dams
designed to prevent the damage and erosion
caused by regular flooding in the southeast,
with the additional benefit of providing hydroelectric power
at a cheap price to a region that lagged behind
the rest of the nation.
The *Rural Electrification Administration* would see to it
that those lacking power throughout the rest of the country
could step into the modern age as well.
The thousands of jobs created
would help to reshape life in rural America.

"Yep;
40 cents an hour
and we were excited about it."

"Were we the greatest generation
or the dumbest generation?"

"What a bunch
of suckers we were.
Give me a cupcake job
like the schmuck writing this book
who gets to sit at a desk and get paid
to make lame jokes all day."

The *National Labor Relations Act* of 1935
outlawed unfair business practices
that gave management the opportunity to exploit labor.
Unions were allowed to bargain collectively for their members
and the right of workers to join a union was guaranteed.
The *National Labor Relations Board* was created to enforce
labor laws and to mediate between labor and management.
In 1938 the **Fair Labor Standards Act**
would restrict child labor, preventing competition
for jobs that would drive wages lower
and preventing children under 16
from having to leave school and work;
would set the maximum work-week at 40 hours,
with time and $\frac{1}{2}$ paid for overtime;
and would establish a nationwide
minimum wage of 40 cents/hour.

"I don't care if I'm getting free money every month;
your music is too loud, you need a haircut,
& when I had to walk to school,
it was uphill both ways, barefoot in the snow."

"And get off my lawn!"

The New Deal program with the greatest and most enduring
impact was likely the *Social Security Act* of 1935.
Prompted by the suggestion of **Dr. Francis Townsend**
to provide a monthly stipend of $200/month to all
senior citizens, the Social Security Act withheld a portion of
workers' paychecks to fund a monthly payment to retirees,
the disabled, and widows & dependent children.
The money spent by recipients not only helped them
to avoid the hardships of poverty, but also pumped money
through the economy to create jobs and support businesses.

"FRANKLIN!!!!!"

"Justice is supposed to be blind, not stupid;
just play by the rules and your time will come."

"For goodness' sake, you're going to be President for pretty much forever;
you'll get to appoint somebody eventually."

Roosevelt's landslide re-election victory over Republican Alf Landon filled the president with sufficient confidence to take on the Supreme Court which had foiled several of his New Deal programs. Frustrated that he had not had an opportunity to name any justices to the Supreme Court during his first term, Roosevelt proposed that he be allowed to nominate an additional justice for any who were older than $70\,{}^{1}\!/_{2}$ years old. This would have allowed FDR to add six additional justices to the Court in the hope of swaying their decisions in a more favorable direction.

In a stinging rebuke of the president, Roosevelt's *court-packing plan* was overwhelmingly rejected, even by fellow Democrats. The perception of an executive power-grab was undeniable, and Roosevelt would see Congress reject a piece of legislation sponsored by him for the first time. As his second term progressed, FDR would have the opportunity to appoint some of his own justices when retirements took place, and the Court began to look more favorably upon Roosevelt's programs throughout the duration of his presidency.

Does it strike anyone as the least bit ironic
that African Americans were discriminated against
for trying to help support a war effort against Nazis?
That we went to war against a country that espoused a "master race"
and enslaved or killed anyone who didn't fit their prototype?
Anyone? Or is it just me?

The Democratic coalition that re-elected FDR
included a significant new component.
For the first time, masses of African Americans abandoned the
party of Lincoln to support the Democratic candidate.
Roosevelt was hesitant, however, to fight the injustices
of discrimination because he felt he still needed the support of
White Democratic congressmen from the South.
One exception to this would come early in Roosevelt's third
term when he issued *Executive Order 8802* which forbade
racial or ethnic discrimination in the defense department
or in the hiring practices of any private defense contractors.
Pressured by African American activists such as
A. Philip Randolph, who threatened to lead
a march on Washington, Roosevelt created
the *Fair Employment Practices Committee* to police violations
of the president's order and to assist African Americans
in finding employment in defense industries as
American participation in World War II loomed on the horizon.

"We're definitely planning on being good neighbors."

"Great neighbors? Let's not get carried away."

'And definitely don't flip ahead about 75 pages
to the part about the Bay of Pigs invasion
or the Iran-Contra Affair."

His hands already full dealing with America's domestic problems, President Roosevelt attempted to keep things placid with the rest of the world. Roosevelt pledged to pursue a *"Good Neighbor" policy* in Latin America, rebuking the Monroe Doctrine and pledging to never again intrude on the sovereign affairs of the nations to our south.

FDR convinced Congress to nullify the *Platt Amendment*, freeing Cuba from all of its onerous conditions save the US base at *Guantanamo Bay*, and also to recognize the Soviet Union as the legitimate government of what had formerly been Russia.

Roosevelt also signed the *Tydings-McDuffie Act* which pledged to return the Philippines to its people as of 1946.

FDR was rightly concerned about the increasing belligerence of Nazi Germany, Mussolini's Italy & Tojo's Japan, but the precarious state of the US economy and the overwhelmingly isolationist beliefs of a majority of Americans restricted his flexibility to act.

As a result of the investigation of the *Nye Commission* which concluded that America's involvement in World War I was due to the American loans and arms sales to the Allies, Congress passed three *Neutrality Acts* in the mid-1930's.

The laws prohibited arms shipments & travel to warring nations; forbade the extension of credit to belligerents; & denied any arms sales to either side in the Spanish Civil War.

"You troublemakers do know
that we haven't ever lost a war yet, right?
Don't be fooled by that War of 1812, either;
it was at worst a tie."

"You do <u>not</u> want to make me
have to cross one of these oceans
to teach you a lesson;"

"You eat dinner too late
and half of you drive
on the wrong side of the road;
I'm going to be all kinds of upset
if I have to come over there
and fix up your messes again."

While Roosevelt would not join the war when Japan attacked
Manchuria or when Germany rolled into Poland,
FDR did his utmost to make sure that the US
would be ready to fight if necessary.
Roosevelt increased defense spending by $^2/_3$ in 1938
and in 1939 ended its arms embargo by agreeing to sell
to the Allies on a *cash & carry* basis. In 1940 Roosevelt signed
the *Selective Service Act*, for the first time preparing for a draft
prior to the initiation of hostilities. 1940 would also see FDR
trade 50 surplus destroyers with England in exchange for eight
Atlantic bases. In March of 1941 as England fought virtually
alone to withstand the Nazi menace, FDR introduced
the *Lend-Lease* program by which the United States
would serve as the *"arsenal of democracy"* and provide
whatever arms the Allies needed in an effort to defeat their
totalitarian foes. In July of 1941, Roosevelt would authorize
US naval escorts for British ships as far as Iceland, and in
September after an attack on the *USS Greer,*
Roosevelt authorized a *"shoot-on-sight"* policy
versus all German naval vessels, essentially entering
into an undeclared war with the Third Reich.

A date that will live
in infamy

On *December 7th, 1941*
353 carrier-borne planes from the Empire of Japan
attacked the US fleet docked at *Pearl Harbor.*
Devastating all eight battleships in port, sinking four,
the Japanese attack killed 2,403 Americans.
Japan had struck pre-emptively to try to knock out American
forces so that Japan could secure oil and rubber resources from
southeast Asia. Japan's attack, while devastating, was the worst
thing it could have done. Japanese forces did no damage to the
huge fuel depots at Pearl Harbor, and all of the US aircraft
carriers were at sea and out of harm's way. Worst of all
for Japan, the most costly attack in US history up to that point
galvanized the will of virtually all Americans to commit the
entirety of our nation to defeating the Japanese aggressor and its
Axis allies. As *Isoroku Yamamoto,*
the commander of the attack predicted,
the Japanese would not lose the war on the field of battle,
but in the factories of Detroit and the oil fields of Oklahoma.
The despicable and stealthy attack would
rouse the sleeping giant, and the United States would emerge
from World War II as the world's lone superpower.

420

Following Congress' declaration of war with but a single dissenting vote, the full military and productive might of the United States would be turned toward the war effort. The *mobilization* of the home front was the deciding factor in the war which would wreak more devastation than any other. More than 5,000,000 women would replace male factory workers sent overseas to fight for their country. *Braceros*, migrant workers from Mexico, were allowed to enter with no restrictions to keep American farms running while they fed people the world over. African Americans fought in the war and stepped up as workers in spite of continued discrimination at work and in the armed forces, waging a *"Double V"* campaign for victory abroad and victory at home.

The *War Production Board* and *Office of War Mobilization* worked to ensure that all resources were oriented toward the battle abroad, with the *Office of Price Administration* rationing goods and setting prices at home. The war would extinguish the unemployment that had plagued the previous decade, with America's factories churning out over 300,000 planes, 100,000 tanks and so many ships that they were being launched faster than the enemy could find and sink them. The *Office of War Information* rallied the nation through propaganda that trumpeted the *Four Freedoms*: *Freedom from Fear, Freedom from Want, Freedom of Speech, & Freedom of Religion* for which we were fighting.

"I pledge allegiance
to the flag
of the United States of America.
And to the republic,
for which it stands
One nation, under God
with Liberty and Justice for all."

One of the greatest injustices perpetrated against Americans during the war was a self-inflicted wound. *Executive Order 8066* allowed the US military to round up and incarcerate 120,000 Japanese-Americans, 70,000 of whom were full US citizens, while others had been residents for decades. These Americans lost their homes and businesses when they were forced from the West Coast to relocation camps hundreds or thousands of miles from home, with no similar imprisonment for Americans of German or Italian ancestry even though we were also at war with those nations. The prisoners were kept in camps with the most meager of amenities and totally restricted from freedom of movement. In spite of this, 33,000 Japanese-Americans volunteered to fight in Europe and the *442nd Regimental Combat Unit* became the most decorated unit in the history of the United States military. The US Supreme Court would uphold this internment of US citizens in violation of their 5th Amendment rights in *Korematsu v. United States*, considered by many scholars to be one of the Court's greatest miscarriages of justice. In 1988, the US government would officially apologize and grant reparations of $20,000 to each American who had been so grievously mistreated.

"But when the admiral said
'island hopping,'
I just naturally assumed…"

"This is so awkward…"

While most Americans lusted for immediate and furious vengeance against Japan, President Roosevelt realized that England was the last impediment to Hitler's blitzkrieg through western Europe. Hitler's great miscalculation would be his betrayal of the secret *Molotov-Ribbentrop Pact* according to which Germany and the USSR would remain at peace. When Stalin brought the Soviet Union into the war on the side of the Allies, Hitler's overconfidence left him fighting on two fronts. However, both Great Britain and the USSR were devastated by the war & were barely hanging on against the German onslaught. Roosevelt and Churchill agreed that the US would focus on the war in Europe first, keeping a pledge to Stalin to open up a second front and take some heat off the overwhelmed Soviet troops. This would lead to a patient strategy in the Pacific for the US. The turning point in the Pacific Theater would be the *Battle of Midway*, where American codebreakers got the better of the Japanese & the US Navy sank four Japanese aircraft carriers, putting the Japanese on the defensive from then on. Admiral *Chester Nimitz* would implement an *"island-hopping"* strategy whereby the US would attack only certain outposts on their way across the Pacific, bypassing strongholds to reach a point from which American planes could bomb Japan. Battles such as *Guadalcanal, Wake Island, Iwo Jima & Okinawa* would put Japan within the range of US forces, & the *Battle of Leyte Gulf* would demolish the remainder of the Japanese Navy.

Contrary to popular opinion,
the 'D' in 'D-Day'
does not stand for
"Damn, that's a lot of ships;
maybe we shouldn't have tried to take over Europe again after all."

The American war for Europe actually began in *North Africa*. Anxious to protect the Suez Canal and the oil resources of the Middle East, General *George Patton* helped the British to defeat German forces in North Africa, from which point Italy could be attacked across the Mediterranean. The Allied invasion of Sicily would shortly lead to Mussolini's demise, but Stalin still clamored for a full-scale assault on the German stronghold in France. Finally, on *June 6th, 1944 Operation Overlord* would commence. Planned by General *Dwight Eisenhower*, the largest invasion in the history of mankind launched across the English Channel.

In the face of dogged resistance, Allied forces established a beachhead at Normandy and by August of 1944 had liberated Paris. The Germans would make a last-ditch attack at the *Battle of the Bulge* in December and January. The stout resistance of the American Army and a last-minute rescue by General Patton ended all hopes for Germany. President Roosevelt would die of a cerebral hemorrhage on April 12th, 1945, but Hitler would commit suicide as Soviet troops took Berlin on April 30th. Germany would surrender unconditionally on May 7th, ending the war in Europe with the Allies victorious.

"*Everybody acted like I was a big teddy-bear when Hitler was still around;*
Now he checks out and all of a sudden
everybody's sending my calls straight to voicemail."

A series of conferences between the Allied leaders would take place throughout World War II.
The *"Big Three"* would meet in one form or another at Casablanca, Tehran, Yalta, and Potsdam.
Casablanca saw Roosevelt and Churchill agree to attack Italy and pursue a policy of ***unconditional surrender*** for Germany.
Tehran was the site where the British & Americans agreed to invade France in the spring of 1944 to relieve pressure on the Soviet forces fighting on the Eastern Front.
Yalta would be Roosevelt's last conference, at which an agreement was reached to divide a conquered Germany between British, American, French & Soviet zones of occupation; to hold free elections in the liberated nations of Central Europe; that the Soviet Union would declare war on Japan within 90 days of the end of fighting in Europe; and that a conference would be held to create a new ***United Nations***.
Stalin would meet with new President *Harry S. Truman* and recently-elected British Prime Minister Clement Atlee at *Potsdam* following Germany's surrender, but the old alliance was already beginning to show strain now that the common enemy had been vanquished.

As many as 85,000,000 people died in World War II, 3% of the world's population at the time.

The world would change forever on *August 6th, 1945*.
The Enola Gay would drop the first ***atomic bomb***
on the Japanese city of ***Hiroshima***. Three days later,
a second bomb would level **Nagasaki**.
The death toll of these two bombs would be
over 250,000 people.
The destructive power of the atom had been unleashed by the
Manhattan Project, a secret US government program in which
over 100,000 people worked under *J. Robert Oppenheimer*
to unleash the power of nuclear fission. President Truman,
who in spite of having been the Vice President and a Senator
before that knew nothing of the $2,000,000,000 project
when he rose to the Oval Office following Roosevelt's death.
Truman had been warned that a conventional invasion
of the Japanese homeland could result in a million casualties for
the United States alone. Truman also feared that Stalin would
demand a say in Japan's post-war rehabilitation,
and he wanted to demonstrate to our erstwhile ally
that we remained a force to be reckoned with.
Truman's decision would lead
to Japan's unconditional surrender
and the end of World War II.

"*Look how great governments have done with individual nations;
If we put them all together, it will be even more successful, right?*"

432

Having learned from our mistake of having chosen
not to join the League of Nations following World War I,
the United States took the lead in fostering
global interconnectedness with the formation
of the **United Nations.**
Meeting at Dunbarton Oaks, Virginia in 1944 representatives of
the United States, Great Britain, the USSR and China
proposed the creation of the global union,
and in April of 1945, delegates from 50 nations gathered
in San Francisco & drafted what would become the UN Charter.
Headquartered in New York on land donated by the Rockefeller
family, the United Nations would consist of a *Security Council*
on which the *US, Great Britain, France, the USSR & China*
would have permanent seats
along with a rotation of other nations.
The five permanent members were to each have *veto* power
over any UN action. The *General Assembly* would have
representatives from every member nation,
and a *Secretary-General* would serve
as a chief executive of the United Nations.
The veto power of the permanent members of the
Security Council would impede the effectiveness of the UN
on many occasions, but the organization has been
a consistent force for good with peacekeeping and
humanitarian missions since its inception in 1945.

"Yeah; I'm reasonably sure this is not what they meant by 'Cold War'."

Contrasting the tenor of peace evoked by the creation of the United Nations was the rapid deterioration of relations between the United States and the Soviet Union. With their common enemy vanquished, hostility between the *democratic, capitalist* United States and the *totalitarian, communist* Soviet Union rapidly became the defining issue of global politics. While Stalin would allow elections in the Soviet-occupied nations of Central Europe, they were hardly "free and fair "as he had pledged at the Yalta Conference. In short order, communist satellite states were emplaced stretching from the Soviet border to East Germany and the Adriatic. Apologists for the Soviets recognized the paranoia that motivated the USSR, given that it had been devastated by two German invasions over a span of less than 30 years, but much of the world feared that a Soviet Union unchecked by the west would foster revolution all over the world in an effort to expand communism. When China's civil war would finally end in 1949 with *Mao Zedong's* communists defeating **Chiang Kai-Shek's** nationalists, the existence of a *Cold War* could not be denied. From 1945 until the collapse of the Soviet Union in 1991, global geopolitics would be driven by the rivalry between the two antithetical philosophies.

"Yes, I'm fully aware that he called it a 'curtain,' but I think that you're missing the point entirely."

Speaking publicly in 1946,
Winston Churchill warned of
"An *Iron Curtain* that has descended across Europe,
stretching from Stettin on the Baltic to Trieste on the Adriatic."
Churchill's speech would play a role in motivating
the nations of the west to eventually form
the *North Atlantic Treaty Organization (NATO)* in 1949.
NATO joined the US and Canada
with ten western European nations in a mutual defense pact
governed by the principle that
"an attack on one was an attack on all."
Membership in NATO would fly in the face of
President Washington's admonition to avoid entangling
alliances, but NATO has endured ever since and helped
to forestall possible Soviet expansion into western Europe.
The communist nations of Eastern Europe would counter the
western alliance in 1955 with the formation of the
Warsaw Pact, which would exist as a counterweight
to NATO until the late 1980's.

"This is really not going to work terribly well."

"China is about to become as red as a fire engine."

"Someone also might want to fire off a memo
to President Trump about this and save him a lot of hassle."

Convinced by diplomat *George Kennan's "Long Telegram,"* President Truman decided in 1947 upon a policy regarding communist expansion that has become known as ***containment.*** This strategy essentially acknowledged the control of the Soviet Union within their already established sphere of influence, but advocated strident resistance to further gains by the communist world. Fearful of a ***domino effect*** of one nation after another falling to communist insurgencies, President Truman implemented the *Truman Doctrine* which stipulated that the United States would provide assistance to any nation threatened by communism from within or without. Truman gained bipartisan support in Congress to send *$400,000,000* in aid to the governments of *Greece & Turkey* which were both teetering precariously in the face of rebel communist factions, but with American aid both remained democratic and both would become member states of NATO.

"Who says money can't buy friends?"

An unmistakable success of US post-war policy was
President Truman's *Marshall Plan*.
Implemented in 1947, the Marshall Plan allotted
$12,000,000,000 to western European nations
ravaged by World War II.
Disbursed over the span of four years, the American aid would
help to stabilize governments across western Europe,
particularly in Italy and France which were struggling with
strong communist parties within their borders.
The aid provided by the United States would foster strong
allegiances among the countries, and much of the money
was spent on American products,
which helped our nation's economy.
The offer of aid was extended to all nations that had suffered
through the war, but the Soviet Union and its satellite states
refused, fearing the impact of American influence.

"Let's kill some Nazis."

*"Because you're eager to get home
and go to college so you can
make a better life
for you and your family
thanks to the new
Servicemen's Readjustment Act
that pays you to learn
out of appreciation for your
selflessness and sacrifice?"*

*"No; because I just like
killing Nazis. They suck."*

Money was also spent generously on the home front,
The *Servicemen's Readjustment Act (GI Bill)* of 1944
provided billions of dollars for veterans to attend college
or trade school upon their return from the war.
The purpose of the GI Bill was two-fold;
not only did it serve as a token of appreciation for the veterans'
service to the nation, but it also helped to ease their transition
back into the workforce which had supplanted them
with other workers during their time overseas.
The GI Bill also provided more than $16,000,000,000
in low-interest loans for veterans
to buy homes and to start businesses.
This infusion of cash helped to stimulate the construction
trades, but the money was not disbursed fairly in all cases,
and minorities were decidedly under-represented in receiving
the government assistance to which they were entitled.

If they had only joined Amazon Prime,
they could have had all of that stuff in just two days.

Truman's resolve would be put to the test in June, 1948
when the Soviets closed all roads and railroads linking
the western sectors of Germany with the corresponding sectors
of Berlin which lay deep within the Soviet sphere.
Though the Soviets were hoping to
provoke a withdrawal by the western powers,
the US and British air forces conducted an 11-month effort to
keep the German capital supplied with food, fuel and medicine.
At the height of the *Berlin Airlift*, a relief flight was landing
every 30 seconds. Ultimately, American and British pilots would
deliver 2,326,406 tons of supplies, nearly two-thirds of which
was coal, on 278,228 flights , flying a total of 92,000,000 miles.
The Soviets finally relented in May of 1949,
but Germany would remain divided between
democratic West Germany and
communist East Germany until 1989
and would serve as a persistent reminder of the tension
between the two competing political and economic systems.

"You've no doubt heard that
'the family that plays together, stays together,' right?"

"Well, apparently
the family that spies together, dies together,'
at least if you're the Rosenbergs."

The post-war paranoia regarding the threat of communism was pervasive at home as well as abroad.

As the United States would find itself increasingly within the grip of a *2nd Red Scare*, personal liberties found themselves threatened on a number of fronts.

The *House Un-American Activities Committee* would seek out alleged communists throughout government and society, leading to compulsory *loyalty oaths* and the *blacklisting* of those deemed uncooperative. Prominent convictions of State Department employee *Alger Hiss* and *Julius & Ethel Rosenberg* would dominate headlines and lead to the execution of the Rosenbergs for having provided atomic secrets to Soviet spies.

Most threatening to even loyal Americans was Wisconsin Senator *Joe McCarthy*. McCarthy used bogus allegations of a communist-riddled State Department to investigate whomever he liked, often threatening uncooperative witnesses with being investigated themselves to coerce their testimony.

The formerly obscure senator would rise to great power and prominence until the *Army-McCarthy hearings* of 1954, during which McCarthy's bullying and dishonest tactics would be revealed during a live television broadcast.

McCarthy's influence would collapse like a house of cards and he would be censured by the Senate, dying of alcoholism three years later.

*"The three years of deadly combat was awful,
but knowing that our sacrifice made BTS possible
makes it all worthwhile."*

The strength of the United States and the mettle of the United Nations would be tested in 1950 when the communist forces of North Korea surged past the *38th Parallel* and invaded South Korea. Mindful of the loss of China to communism the year prior, President Truman called on the United Nations to step up to South Korea's defense. With the USSR boycotting the Security Council in protest of *Taiwan* maintaining China's seat subsequent to the 1949 revolution, the US was able to lead a United Nations *"police action"* in defense of South Korea. General *Douglas MacArthur* was put in charge of UN forces, although the troops were overwhelmingly American, and conducted a daring raid at *Inchon* behind the enemy's lines. MacArthur's daring strategy turned the tide, and UN forces drove toward the *Yalu River* with the intention of defeating the North Koreans and unifying the Korean peninsula. Ignoring Truman's orders and China's threat to attack, MacArthur pushed forward, and when Chinese troops retaliated, the *Korean War* reached a dangerous stalemate, which would eventually last until the present day, with only an *armistice* but no final resolution. MacArthur's disregarding of Truman's orders would lead to his firing, but it would take until after the election of *Dwight D. Eisenhower* for even a tenuous peace to come to the Korean people.

"If we have to kill them to save them, so be it;"

"Better to die free than to live under Godless communism."

The election of President Eisenhower would lead to a change in strategies regarding how to deal with the threat of communism. Truman's policy of containment would be replaced by *Massive Retaliation*, a strategy developed by Secretary of State *John Foster Dulles*. Massive Retaliation focused on the threat of a US nuclear response as a deterrent to communist aggression around the world. When the USSR also gained access to nuclear weapons in 1954, the threat to respond to any crisis with such an extreme response became a recipe for mutual annihilation. Strategic nuclear forces were supposed to be a cheaper alternative to costly conventional troops and weapons, but the inflexibility of response options left the US with its hands tied when dealing with less-than existential threats. The concept of *Mutually-Assured Destruction (MAD)* would govern US-Soviet relations over the next 40 years. Although outright war never broke out between the two rival nations, the *brinkmanship* of the era brought the world closer to the end of civilization than at any time in human history.

"Oh, look honey; the houses are all white, just like the people living in them."

452

The post-war era would see tremendous demographic changes in the United States. Flush with cash saved during the war and subsidized by the FHA and the GI Bill, the Americans known as *Baby-Boomers* began to abandon the cities and flock to the suburbs. Developers gobbled up farmland on the outskirts of cities which, thanks to the abundance of automobiles and massive governmental support for highway construction, would become *suburbs* beckoning to America's middle-class.

If you were White.

Long Island's *Levittown*, a development of 17,000 homes built outside New York City, characterized the new communities. Bungalows, split-levels and ranch houses would dominate pastoral neighborhoods where each family could have their own yard in which to play and barbecue. However, many of these developments refused to sell to non-Whites, and as Whites fled to the suburbs, aging cities lost much of their tax base and city services suffered, as many cities became derelict and dangerous. Paralleling this movement from city to suburb was a migration from northeast to southwest. The *"sun belt"* became wildly popular as Americans sought to abandon the decrepit cities and bad weather of America's industrial heartland.

This transition continues to the present day, even as the resources of the South and West are overtaxed by their increased populations.

Finally, it was only the ball that had to be white.

America's pastime would shake the core of historic segregation when *Jackie Robinson* took the field for the Brooklyn Dodgers in 1947. This was not Robinson's first time standing up to discrimination. As a 2nd Lieutenant in the Army, Robinson had been court-martialed for refusing to move to the back of a non-segregated military bus while stationed in Texas. Robinson would eventually be acquitted, but his greatest fame would come when despite death threats, hostility from both opposing players and even some of his own teammates, and having to live and eat in separate accommodations from the other players, Robinson would not only be named Rookie of the Year, but would be a six-time All-Star, a Most Valuable Player, a World Series champion and a member of the Major League Baseball Hall of Fame. In 1997, Major League Baseball would retire Robinson's #42 jersey throughout the sport as a tribute to his trailblazing greatness. Following shortly after Robinson's bold step, *President Truman* would order *the full integration of the US Armed Forces*, striking a further blow against racial discrimination.

"Well, the board has always been black, so it's not like we're racists or anything."

A triumph for the racial equality of all Americans occurred in 1954 when the Supreme Court unanimously overturned the 1896 *Plessy v. Ferguson* decision in *Brown v. Board of Education*. NAACP lawyer *Thurgood Marshall*, who would himself go on to become the first African American Justice to sit on the US Supreme Court, led a team that convinced Chief Justice *Earl Warren* to declare emphatically that *"separate but equal is inherently unequal"* and that segregation in schools should be eliminated *"with all deliberate speed."*

Resistance would be swift and violent, with 101 members of Congress signing a *"Southern Manifesto"* condemning the Court's decision. Governor *Orval Faubus* would use the Arkansas National Guard to prevent Black students from attending Little Rock High School, and President Eisenhower had to send in the 101st Airborne Division to make sure that the *"Little Rock Nine"* could attend school.

Air Force veteran *James Meredith* would need US Marshals to attend the University of Mississippi, and even in the North, massive resistance to integration would persist for decades. White students fled integrated schools, and despite the Court's clear ruling, to this day, most American children attend schools with very little diversity.

Sometimes taking a stand means taking a seat

Civil rights icon *Rosa Parks* would help to advance the fight against discrimination in 1955 when she refused to move to the back of a Montgomery, Alabama bus. 75% of Montgomery's bus riders were African American, but when four White passengers were standing at the front of the bus, the driver opened up the front rows of the "colored section" for the white passengers. Parks refused to give up her seat and was arrested. Reverend *Martin Luther King Jr.* would rocket to national prominence when he helped to organize the Montgomery Bus Boycott to protest this injustice. Modeling his strategies on the example of Henry David Thoreau's concept of *civil disobedience*, Dr. King and the *Southern Christian Leadership Conference* would organize car pools, rent vans, raise money for fines and walk alongside thousands of Black citizens, until the financial losses for the Montgomery Bus Line were so pronounced that segregation on busses was ended after 381 days.

"Think Americans will never be dumber?"

"Just wait until the internet is invented."

As the nation entered the 1950's,
fewer than 20% of American households had a *television*.
By 1960, over 90% of homes had at least one TV.
National networks ABC, NBC, & CBS broadcast on 530 local
stations, bringing news, sports and entertainment to
a nationwide audience. Families clustered around the television
and a national culture spread from coast-to-coast.
Most shows were in black & white,
and stations typically went off the air
between midnight and 6 AM,
but the nation remained transfixed by the television
no matter how vacuous and insipid the programs were.
TV would impact the course of the nation as millions watched
Nixon debate Kennedy;
stayed riveted during the Cuban Missile Crisis;
mourned collectively during the assassinations
of the Kennedys and Dr. King;
and as body after body came back from the jungles of Vietnam.
And the commercials. Lots and lots of commercials.
FCC Chairman Newton Minnow would christen television
"a vast wasteland,"
but viewership continued to grow year after year.

"Thank you;
Thank you very much."

"And whatever you do,
don't Google how I died."

With its roots in African American rhythms found in
jazz and the blues, the 1950's would see the emergence
of a distinctly American music that would capture the attention
of the world and panic parents across the country.
Rock & Roll would upend musical sensibilities among
White America about what music could be.
Crossover stars like *Chuck Berry* and *Little Richard*
would find their musical styles and even their songs exposed to
a wider mainstream audience by artists like Bill Haley,
Buddy Holly and Jerry Lee Lewis, but the biggest star of the
1950's would undoubtedly be *Elvis Presley*.
Although tame by contemporary standards,
Presley's performances were deemed so provocative
that broadcasters would only film his TV performances
from the waist up.
Although certainly derivative and culturally appropriative,
rock & roll would dominate American music for decades
and influence popular culture the world over.

The most routinely-ignored sign in America,
except by those senior citizens in the passing lane
whose left-turn signal has been on for the last 14 miles

1956 would see President Eisenhower sign into law the
National Interstate and Defense Highways Act.
At an original price-tag of $25,000,000,000 the plan to construct
41,000 miles of toll-free modern high-speed freeways connecting
all major cities in the United States was the costliest endeavor
ever pursued by the federal government.
Inspired by a nightmarish cross-country military convoy
Eisenhower had taken part in after World War I and the
autobahns he had witnessed in Germany,
the Interstate Highway System would
revolutionize travel and commerce in the United States.
Passenger rail service would be decimated by the opportunity to
travel even more quickly on one's own schedule in the comfort of
one's own car. Increased connectivity would facilitate the
expansion of suburbs as workers could now more easily
commute to work in the city while still enjoying the bucolic
benefits of lives lived outside of them, at great cost to America's
urban centers. While the highways have undoubtedly enhanced
the quality of life for millions of commuters, the impact of lives
lost in high-speed accidents and the environmental impact
of ribbons of concrete traversed by millions of cars each day has
taken a significant toll on all of the United States.

True, the Soviets were the first to put a satellite into space,
but while they were fooling around with that,
it was an American who invented the Hula Hoop,
so suck on that, Boris

America uttered a collective gasp on October 4th, 1957
when the Soviet Union successfully launched *Sputnik*,
the first artificial satellite ever put into orbit.
Over a three-month span, Sputnik would circle the Earth
1,440 times covering a total of 43,000,000 miles
at a speed of 18,000 miles per hour.
Weighing only 184 pounds and measuring just 23 inches in
circumference, Sputnik filled Americans' hearts with dread.
The ability of the Soviets to launch a satellite,
something the United States had yet to accomplish,
meant that the USSR could also launch nuclear-tipped missiles
capable of reaching the United States.
Sputnik's launch would start a *"Space Race"* in which the US
would struggle to keep up, as the Soviets would also become
the first to launch a man into orbit a few years later.
The US would continue to lag behind until the *Apollo* program
of the 1960's would see the United States become
the first country to land a person on the moon.
Sputnik would be the impetus behind Congress passing the
National Defense and Education Act, which would fund
increases in engineering, math and the sciences
in an effort to facilitate the closure of the *missile gap*
that threatened the perceived safety of the United States.

"Yankee, go home."

*"After you leave the cash,
of course."*

The Soviet Union would find itself posing a more proximal threat to the United States when a revolutionary movement in *Cuba* that had been simmering throughout the post-war years boiled over in 1959 and a communist government led by *Fidel Castro* toppled the US-friendly Fulgencio Batista. Castro's Marxist one-party rule was problematic for US business interests in neighboring Cuba, so on April 16th, 1961 a brigade of 1,400 Cuban expatriates trained and supplied by the CIA attempted to land and overthrow Castro at the *Bay of Pigs*. The clumsy invasion was quickly routed, and 1,189 revolutionaries were captured and put on trial. Castro would end up ransoming them for $25,000,000 in medicine and supplies, but newly-elected President *John F. Kennedy* and the United States were made to look foolish and incompetent.

"Remember when cigars
were the most dangerous things
to come out of Cuba?"

"I sure miss
the good old days."

The world would come as close to annihilation as it ever has during the *Cuban Missile Crisis.*
Over a 35-day span in October and November of 1962.
U-2 reconnaissance planes revealed the construction of Soviet medium-range ballistic missile launchers on Cuba, only 90 miles from the United States. A tense confrontation ensued when President Kennedy issued a naval *"quarantine"* around the island, carefully skirting the use of the term "blockade" which would have been an act of war.
Cooler heads finally prevailed when the USSR agreed to remove the missiles from Cuba in exchange for an American pledge not to attempt another invasion of Cuba and a promise to remove
American nuclear missiles from Turkey.
The crisis averted, the US and the Soviet Union would establish a direct *"hot-line"* between the leaders of the two nations in an attempt to let diplomacy prevent military escalation should future crises occur.

"Why is this big hole here?"

"It's no wonder people
have been escaping."

On August 13th, 1961 the government of East Germany
began construction of the *Berlin Wall*,
which would come to symbolize the schism of the Cold War.
Prior to its construction, 3,500,000 East Germans had escaped to
freedom in the West. East Germany claimed that the wall had
been built to prevent fascist incursions into their country,
but the reality was that the communist ideal promoted by the
totalitarian state was driving its own people toward capitalism
and democracy. Between 1961 and the fall of the wall
on November 9th, 1989 only 5,000 East Germans would
successfully evade the lethal defenses flanking the wall,
while over 200 would be killed trying.
President Kennedy showed the support of the United States
for the German people, famously declaring
"Ich bin ein Berliner" when he visited the wall
to decry its construction.

"Let every nation know, whether it wishes us well or ill,
that we shall pay any price, bear any burden, meet any hardship,
support any friend, oppose any foe,
in order to assure the survival and the success of liberty ."

On November 22nd, 1963
President *John F. Kennedy* would be shot and killed by
Lee Harvey Oswald in Dallas, Texas.
Oswald would himself be shot and killed two days later by
Jack Ruby during a jail transfer, and conspiracy theories would
flourish as to whether Oswald acted alone
and who might have been behind the assassination.
Both the specially-convened *Warren Commission* and
the *House Select Committee on Assassinations*
concluded that Oswald acted alone.
Vice President *Lyndon Johnson* would succeed Kennedy,
whose youth and charisma had charmed the nation and
renewed national confidence that the United States was moving
forward toward a *"New Frontier."* Sadness over Kennedy's
assassination masked the fact that he had not been
especially successful in moving the Democratic agenda forward,
had done little for civil rights
and had increased US involvement in Vietnam.

"I've been to the mountaintop..."
"I've looked over and I've seen the promised land."
"I may not get there with you,
but I want you to know tonight
that we as a people will get to the promised land."

The 1960's would see great strides made in the
battle for racial equality. Reverend *Martin Luther King Jr.'s*
continued leadership would be most evident in 1963's
March on Washington, in which over 200,000 Americans
heard his famous *"I Have a Dream"* speech calling for
an end to prejudice and discrimination.
President Lyndon Johnson, a far more experienced and effective
politician than his predecessor, was able to push through the
24th Amendment which barred poll taxes,
and the *Voting Rights Act of 1965* would end literacy tests and
mandate federal supervision of voting
in areas of Black voter suppression.
Perhaps most impactful was the *Civil Rights Act of 1964*
which outlawed racial segregation in all establishments
open to the public. The creation of the
Equal Employment Opportunity Commission
allowed the federal government to prosecute
discrimination in hiring and in the workplace.
Dr. King would win the Nobel Peace Prize for his efforts in 1964,
but like President Kennedy before him, would be struck dead by
an assassin's bullet when he was murdered in 1968 by
James Earl Ray. Dr. King's death, and the assassination of
Senator *Bobby Kennedy* the same year, made many question
whether the United States could ever truly become
one nation, under God, with liberty and justice for all.

"It is a time for martyrs now, and if I am to be one,
it will be for the cause of brotherhood. "
"That's the only thing that can save this country."

Contrasting the non-violent protests of Dr. King,
other civil rights activists embraced the belief of Marcus Garvey
that separation from White America was the only chance
African Americans had for justice.
Stokely Carmichael, the leader of the
Student Nonviolent Coordinating Committee (SNCC)
advocated for *Black Power*, and the *Black Panthers*
led by *Huey Newton & Bobby Seale*
encouraged armed resistance to racist oppression.
The 1960's would be characterized by an increasing level of
violence on the parts of both White and Black Americans,
from the assault on *Freedom Riders* ordered by
Birmingham Commissioner of Public Safety *"Bull" Connor*
to the violent attacks on the *Edmund Pettis Bridge*
that brutalized marchers calling for voting rights
to riots in the *Watts* neighborhood of Los Angeles
and dozens of other major American cities.
Most influential was likely *Malcolm X*,
a leader in the *Nation of Islam* who advocated for change
"by any means necessary."
He would come to moderate his views somewhat after
becoming disillusioned with the Black Muslim movement,
but would be assassinated in 1965
by members of the group that he had left behind.

*"We are not about to send American boys
nine or ten thousand miles away from home
to do what Asian boys ought to be doing for themselves."*

LYNDON B. JOHNSON

The quagmire of American military involvement in *Vietnam* began when the French withdrew from Indochina in 1954. Vietnam was divided at the 17th Parallel pending an election intended to determine the nature of its government. The elections never took place as it was feared that *Ho Chi Minh's* communist party would emerge victorious. The United States would provide South Vietnam's corrupt government with over $1,000,000,000 over the next six years, but little progress was made. President Kennedy increased the US commitment and sent over 16,000 military "advisors," but the real commitment occurred under President Lyndon Johnson. As a result of a perceived attack on a US vessel, Congress passed the *Tonkin Gulf Resolution* in 1964 authorizing Johnson to do whatever he deemed necessary to guard the nation's interest in Vietnam. By 1969, the US would have 540,000 troops stationed in Vietnam waging an increasingly unpopular war. The combination of the war in Vietnam and domestic instability would lead Johnson to choose not to run for re-election. President *Richard Nixon* would expand bombing into *Laos & Cambodia*, but would follow a process called "*Vietnamization*" by which US financial support would continue while US troops were brought home. South Vietnam would fall in April of 1975. In 1973, the *War Powers Act* would be passed over Nixon's veto which would prohibit future presidents from such unconstrained aggression.

"These rulings tie one hand
behind my back,
and I've only _got_ one!"

"What is wrong with this cartoonist?"

Seldom has an era witnessed a greater expansion of individual rights in the United States than the 1960's.
Chief Justice *Earl Warren* would lead the Court to rule on a number of consequential issues involving the rights of citizens versus the power of the government.

Mapp v. Ohio made illegally-obtained evidence inadmissible; *Gideon v. Wainwright & Escobedo v. Illinois* guaranteed legal representation to anyone standing trial; *Miranda v. Arizona* mandated that police inform anyone being arrested of their constitutional rights; *Engel v. Vitale* outlawed mandatory prayer in school; and *Griswold v. Connecticut* forbid restrictions on contraceptives, guaranteeing a right of privacy under the 14th Amendment.

"Wow,
they must have really been serious
when they said that
'all Americans
shall have medical coverage!'"

The 1960's were a period of great social upheaval. *Betty Friedan's* <u>*Feminine Mystique*</u> helped motivate millions of women to demand equal rights in the workplace and in society. The *National Organization for Women (NOW)* fought for the *Equal Pay Act* of 1963 and for *Title IX* in 1973 which made gender discrimination in schools illegal, although the *Equal Rights Amendment* remains unratified. *Cesar Chavez* would help the *United Farm Workers* movement to organize and assist migrant farmworkers in the Southwest, while the *American Indian Movement (AIM)* would agitate for fair treatment and compensation for Native Americans.

The *Stonewall Uprising* in 1969 would begin a movement by LGBTQ+ Americans for equal protection and equal access that continues to this day.

The *Immigration Act of 1965* would finally eliminate nation-of-origin as a criteria for immigrating to the United States.

The *Elementary & Secondary Education Act* would provide federal money for impoverished school districts, but the most impactful *Great Society* program was the establishment of *Medicare & Medicaid*, which provided healthcare for the elderly and the poor, respectively.

"It's a good thing that these cars are being built safer,
because since the pill got here,
there's been a lot more attention paid to what's going on
in the back seat than what's happening in the front."

In the tradition of the muckrakers who brought about social change in the Progressive Era, a number of advocates broke through the popular consciousness during the 1960's.

1962 saw the publication of *Rachel Carson's Silent Spring* in which she alerted readers to the dangers of chemicals such as *DDT* that were harming the environment.

William Masters & Virginia Johnson's pioneering research on human sexuality published in *Human Sexual Response* normalized sexuality for many Americans, and the introduction of the *birth control pill* led to greater empowerment for women and a conspicuous loosening of American mores.

Ralph Nader published *Unsafe at any Speed* in which he detailed the dangers inherent in American automobiles due to automakers emphasizing profits versus safety improvements, and would lead to innovations such as the seat belt and puncture-resistant gas tanks that have saved countless lives.

"Well, maybe all we <u>need</u> is love,
but a shower and some deodorant and maybe a job
might be something that some of us could really use too."

The *counterculture* movement of the late 1960's
would be rooted in a fringe rejection of traditional values,
but would go on to have an outsized impact on American society
that has resonated through subsequent decades.
The *sexual revolution*, rock music, and experimentation with
drugs such as marijuana and LSD became almost mainstream
among much of America's youth, and support for the civil rights
movement coupled with resistance to the Vietnam War
would make these youngsters front-page news.
Students for a Democratic Society issued the
Port Huron Statement calling for dramatic change,
while *Yippies* such as *Abbie Hoffman* and the
Weather Underground became more radicalized and fought
against government oppression and injustice, most notably
at the *Democratic Convention of 1968* in Chicago.
When leaders such as *Timothy Leary* called for teens to
"Turn on, tune in, and drop out,"
many more conservative Americans, Nixon's *"Silent Majority,"*
yearned for the comfort and security of more traditional times.
When more than 400,000 people showed up for
"Three Days of Peace & Love" at the *Woodstock* rock festival,
many Americans felt that our nation
had reached a turning point.
Which direction it would head would remain to be seen.

"Wait, take another one; I think I blinked."

Although President Kennedy wouldn't live
to see his promise fulfilled,
on July 20th, 1969 *Apollo 11* astronauts
Neil Armstrong & Buzz Aldrin
took *"a giant leap for mankind"* when they
set foot on the moon, returning safely four days later
with fellow astronaut Michael Collins
having accomplished what no person ever had.
The *NASA* space program would achieve numerous triumphs
since its creation, and continues to lead both American
and international investigation of the universe around us,
and research related to the space program has improved
life on Earth in countless ways.

"This war has already stretched the generation gap so wide that it threatens to pull the country apart."
Senator Frank Church —May 13, 1970.

Anti-war protests would turn violent at *Kent State* University
in Ohio and Mississippi's *Jackson State* University.
On May 4th, 1970, approximately 2,000 protestors gathered
at Kent State to voice their objections to Nixon's announcement
that the war had been extended into Cambodia.
An ROTC building was burned, and as students confronted
National Guard troops sent to maintain order,
shots killed four students and wounded nine others.
Ten days later at Jackson State, two students were killed and
twelve wounded when police opened fire in a dormitory
shortly after midnight.
The violence at these and other campuses regarding the war
in Vietnam and the draft which was helping to sustain it would
help to convince Americans to ratify the *26th Amendment*
which would give 18, 19, & 20 year-olds the right to vote for the
government that was forcing them against their will
to fight a war they did not support.

"People have got to know whether or not their president is a crook.
Well, I'm not a crook."
"Because to be a crook you would need to have been convicted,
and I got a full pardon from President Ford
for any and all crimes I may have committed when I was President."
"And just because I named him vice president and then he pardoned me
before I was even charged does not mean
that there was any kind of cover-up."
"It might just be a weird coincidence; you don't know."

After having lost the 1960 presidential election to
John F. Kennedy, few expected *Richard Nixon* to again appear
on the national stage. However, increasing dissatisfaction with
President Lyndon Johnson's inability to fully implement his
Great Society domestic agenda while also successfully
resolving the war in Vietnam led many Americans to turn to the
former vice president, and in 1968, Nixon would defeat
Democratic candidate Hubert Humphrey and enter the
White House with the support of the *"silent majority"* of
Americans who feared change, who resented the civil rights and
anti-war movements, and who wanted an aggressive
anti-communist foreign policy that would win the war.
While Nixon would be responsible for many impressive
achievements ranging from thawing tensions with China
to signing an antiballistic missile treaty and a strategic arms
limitation treaty with the Soviet Union to establishing the EPA,
Nixon's overall record is one worthy of condemnation.
Nixon's *"southern strategy"* would finally bring White
southern voters into the Republican coalition by opposing
most civil rights legislation and focusing on fundamentalist
social issues. President Nixon would illegally expand the war in
southeast Asia into *Laos & Cambodia*, and worst of all,
Nixon's cover-up of the *Watergate* scandal would lead to his
resignation from the presidency in order to forestall
almost-certain impeachment.

*"Admittedly, Watergate was not a good look
and Nixon was a paranoid, alcoholic racist,
but he did get us Ling-Ling & Hsing-Hsing;
that's got to count for something."*

Nixon's credentials as an avowed anti-communist were well-established, going back to his days as a leading member of the House Un-American Activities Committee during the 2nd Red Scare. As such, his willingness to seek an easing of tensions with the USSR and China could be tolerated by conservative Americans suspicious that a Democratic president might be giving in to the nation's rivals. Nixon and his Secretary of State *Henry Kissinger* implemented a policy of *"détente"* by which they hoped to bring a thaw to the Cold War. Nixon saw an opportunity to play the Soviet Union and China against one another after an ideological split, and made the world a safer place when the US and the USSR negotiated a reduction in nuclear missiles in the *SALT Treaty* and limits on defensive missile emplacements in the *ABM Treaty*.

Nixon would lay the groundwork for establishing diplomatic relations with communist China through a ping-pong competition between the two nations which would lead to Nixon visiting China himself and the Chinese government giving two panda bears to the US as a gift.

Most significantly, Nixon would lay the groundwork for the US withdrawal from the Vietnam War in 1973, although two years later South Vietnam would fall to the communists and the loss of 58,000 American lives and over 1 trillion dollars would prove to have been in vain.

"You're just being melodramatic;
the environment is fine.
The EPA is just another example of
deep-state, federal bureaucratic
overreach…"

The *Environmental Protection Agency (EPA)* would be formed in 1970 to address how our government could safeguard the nation and the world for future generations, and the *Clean Air Act* & *Clean Water Act* would immeasurably improve the quality of life for Americans.
The *Endangered Species Act* was passed in 1973 to protect animals threatened by potential extinction, saving America's symbol, the bald eagle, which nearly died out due to *DDT* weakening the eggs they laid.
In 1979, a near-meltdown at the *Three Mile Island* nuclear power plant in Pennsylvania would call attention to the threat posed by nuclear power and the radioactive waste it generated, and billions of dollars would be dedicated to a *"superfund"* to clean up dangerously contaminated industrial waste sites.

"Next time,
let me pick the plumbers."

The *Watergate* scandal is arguably the worst political scandal in United States history, and did a great deal of harm to the confidence of the American people that their government could be trusted to abide by the laws it was established to enforce. Prior to the 1972 election, President Nixon, although popular in the polls and highly likely to be re-elected, gave in to his characteristic paranoia and allowed subordinates to coordinate a "dirty tricks" campaign to smear political opponents and to use the IRS and the FBI to investigate potential adversaries.

A group called *"the Plumbers"* hired by the *Committee to Re-Elect the President (CREEP)* was caught burglarizing the Democratic National Headquarters. While it is not altogether certain that Nixon ordered the break-in, it became clear that Nixon was involved in the attempted cover-up. 26 administration officials would be sentenced to jail when a hidden set of audiotapes confirmed Nixon's complicity.

Nixon fought the subpoena for the tapes for months citing executive privilege, but when that failed, even though significant portions of the tapes had been erased in the interest of "national security," Nixon's participation was confirmed and his character indelibly tarnished. When Nixon fired the special prosecutor leading the investigation & the House Judiciary Committee voted three articles of impeachment for abuse of power, contempt of Congress & obstruction of justice, Nixon resigned. Nixon would be pardoned by *Gerald Ford*, his hand-picked successor, & the nation's cynicism compounded.

Go ahead;
<u>You</u> come up with a funny cartoon
about abortion.
I'll wait …

1973 would see the Supreme Court reach one of its most controversial decisions with its 7-2 decision in *Roe v. Wade*. The Burger Court determined that a right to privacy guaranteed by the 14th Amendment extended to a woman's right to choose what to do with her own body, and that state laws restricting abortion were unconstitutional. The decision would galvanize resistance from abortion foes, and form an unlikely coalition between evangelical Protestants and Catholics who would go on to form a conservative bloc that would focus on social issues to the present day and have an outsized influence upon the Republican Party.

Subsequent court decisions including *Planned Parenthood v. Casey* would erode access to abortion, implementing a viability cutoff and allowing restrictions such as a mandatory waiting period and parental notification if minors wanted an abortion.

Social protests on both sides of the issue would continue to the present day, with a woman's right to choose remaining one of the nation's most controversial issues.

Originally proposed in 1923, the *Equal Rights Amendment* was officially passed by Congress in 1971.
Patterned on the 14th Amendment that guaranteed due process of law and citizenship rights regardless of race, the ERA offered the same protections regarding gender. Although it received strong bipartisan support and the support of Presidents Nixon, Ford & Carter, by 1977 the ERA had been ratified by only 35 of the 38 states necessary for it to pass. Congress extended the window for ratification until 1982, but in 1979 five states rescinded their ratifications and the ERA failed to become law. Opponents of ratification were led by *Phyllis Schlafly*, a conservative activist who stoked fear by claiming that the ERA would open women up to being drafted into the military, that it would eliminate alimony, and that it would end the preference typically given to women regarding child custodial rights.
Nevada, Illinois & Virginia would ratify the ERA between 2017-2020, but as of 2022 women are still not Constitutionally protected against gender discrimination.

"$1.31 a gallon!?!"

"I just want to buy the gas, not the whole gas station."

(This will generate absolutely no outrage in those of you
who are driving in 2022. Especially you Tesla drivers.)

In 1973, the *Organization of Petroleum Exporting Countries (OPEC)* decided to embargo the sale of oil to the United States due to our support of Israel in the Yom Kippur War.
Gas prices shot up from 36¢/ gallon in 1972 to $1.31/gallon in 1981.
These price increases contributed to an economic crisis in which the nation would end up experiencing significant inflation concurrently with high unemployment, a new phenomenon economists dubbed "*stagflation.*"
The high gas prices would hurt GDP generally and the automotive sector specifically as car buyers pivoted from gas-guzzling American models to more fuel efficient imports, most notably from Japan. President Nixon would make an unpopular decision to lower interstate highway speeds to 55 mph in an effort to conserve fuel, but the oil crisis would continue to plague the United States for several more years.
An unintended benefit of the oil crisis would be a reduction in air pollution as Americans drove more fuel efficient cars.

It wouldn't be all sunshine and unicorns after this;
Israel remains at odds with the Palestinians, Iran, Syria
and terrorist groups including Hamas, Hezbollah, ISIS & Al-Qaeda.
I think they're going to need a whole bunch more doves.

The 1976 presidential election would see incumbent *Gerald Ford*, having faced down a strong challenge from *Ronald Reagan* in the Republican primary, run against Democratic Governor *Jimmy Carter* of Georgia. Carter ran as a Washington outsider, and the nation's voters, tired of the Watergate scandal, the failure of the Vietnam War, and disillusioned by the unrealized promise of the 1960's elected Carter. Carter's presidency would be regarded as a failure by most Americans. Plagued by a faltering economy, an energy crisis, the taking of 56 American hostages by Iranian revolutionaries and a disheartened nation, Carter would serve only a single term. A kind, generous and spiritual man, Carter would live for decades as likely our most accomplished ex-president, widely admired for his charity and moral leadership. A standout exception to Carter's struggles as president was his facilitation of the *Camp David Accords*. In 1978, Carter would bring together President *Anwar Sadat* of Egypt and Israeli Prime Minister *Menachem Begin*. The three men would share the Nobel Peace Prize for bringing about the first recognition of Israel by an Arab state, in exchange for Israel returning to Egypt the Sinai Peninsula which had been captured in the Six-Day War. The peace between Israel and Egypt has lasted to the present day, and has paved the way for an easing of tensions between Israel and several other Arab states, which has made the historically volatile Middle East region significantly more stable over the ensuing years.

"All I'm saying is that as of January 20th, there's going to be a new sheriff in town and it's not going to take him too long to figure out which missile is pointed right at Tehran, so you might want to think about getting us on a flight back home right away."

"The peanut farmer has left the building. and Reagan does <u>NOT</u> play around."

Jimmy Carter's greatest failure as president was unquestionably his failure to resolve the *Iran Hostage Crisis*.

The CIA had facilitated a coup in Iran in 1953 which empowered *Mohamed Reza Pahlavi* as Shah. The Shah was a secular leader who was friendly to the US and who provided the United States with a reliable ally in the Middle East and, most important, a steady flow of oil. When *Shi'ite* fundamentalists led by *Ayatollah Ruhollah Khomeini* overthrew the Shah, the US allowed him to enter the country to receive cancer treatments. In retaliation, Iranian students breached the US embassy in Tehran and took dozens of Americans hostage, 52 of whom would be held for 444 days. President Carter would eventually attempt a military rescue, but when a helicopter crashed into a transport plane, eight Americans were killed and the plan had to be aborted. Carter's inability to resolve the crisis left the United States looking weak and impotent, and would be a key factor in Carter losing the 1980 election to *Ronald Reagan*. The hostages would not be released until after Reagan's inauguration on January 20th, 1981 as a final insult toward President Carter.

"Government is not the solution to our problem;
government is the problem.."
Ronald Reagan, 1st Inaugural Address

President *Ronald Reagan's* election in 1980 concluded a transition among the American electorate that had begun in the 1930's. Reagan won over 90% of the electoral votes in 1980 by bringing southern white conservatives and white working-class voters into the conservative coalition that has endured to the present day.

Reagan's optimistic outlook and reassuring tone spoke to many Americans who longed for the "good old days" before the Vietnam War, the social unrest of the civil rights era, and the economic misery of stagflation.

During the campaign, Reagan's question "are you better off than you were four years ago?" resonated with his base, and his emphasis on deregulation, strong support for the military and reducing taxes allowed him to maintain high levels of popularity throughout his two terms in office. Reagan's coattails would carry fellow Republicans to success and they would take control of the Senate for the first time in decades.

Reagan declared that it was *"morning in America,"* and although his tenure would include a serious recession in 1982 and a major scandal with the *Iran/Contra Affair*, Reagan remains one of the nation's most beloved presidents due to his affability, his confidence and his ability to connect with his fellow Americans and make them feel good about our nation.

"With the brilliance of this economic plan,
my services certainly won't be required here."

True to his Republican nature, President Reagan would implement the same economic philosophy as Presidents Harding, Coolidge & Hoover during the 1920's, President George W. Bush during the early 2000's, and President Donald Trump from 2016-2020.

Supply-side economics (Reagonomics) focuses on cutting taxes on the wealthy and on businesses, in the belief that the money that would otherwise have gone to the government will be utilized to invest in production, with more jobs being created and the benefits "trickling-down" to the poor and middle-class.

While this sounds good in practice, it has never worked. The wealthy have tended to invest in stocks rather than in creating jobs, and businesses have historically repurchased their own stock to drive up its value rather than in expanding their productivity. Each time this policy has been tried, economic problems have ensued. After the 1920's, the Great Depression followed. During the Reagan administration, the national debt tripled from under $1 trillion to nearly $3 trillion. The Bush administration was followed by the Great Recession of 2007-2010, and the Trump administration saw the national debt surpass $30 trillion thanks to a lowering of corporate taxes and taxes on the very wealthy. *Trickle-Down economics* has always only been a ploy by the rich and powerful to maintain the status quo, and the chasm between them and everyone else has only swollen.

Probably not what Reagan was thinking,
but intimidating nonetheless

One accomplishment for which President Reagan certainly deserves a great deal of credit is his helping to bring about the collapse of America's long-time rival, the Soviet Union. President Reagan would throw American support behind the *Mujahedeen* resistance that fought back against Soviet aggression following their invasion of *Afghanistan* in 1979. More significantly, Reagan greatly expanded military spending, compelling our Soviet rivals to try to keep up, which their economy could not sustain. The greatest contributor to this arms race was Reagan's *Strategic Defense Initiative*, more commonly known as *"Star Wars."*
The SDI consisted of a substantial investment in still unproven space-based weapons like lasers and killer satellites.
The attempt by the Soviet Union to match
US efforts to militarize space would lead new Soviet leader *Mikhail Gorbachev* to restructure the Soviet political and economic systems. Gorbachev even proposed that both the US and the USSR should eliminate their nuclear arsenals and abandon their advanced space-weapon programs.
Reagan's rejection of these proposals and the subsequent collapse of the USSR without a full-blown war between the United States and what Reagan deemed *"the Evil Empire"* stands as a tremendous accomplishment for President Reagan.

"In spite of the wildly speculative and false stories of arms for hostages and alleged ransom payments, we did not—repeat, did not—trade weapons or anything else for hostages, nor will we."

President Ronald Reagan, November 1986

"A few months ago, I told the American people I did not trade arms for hostages. My heart and my best intentions still tell me that's true, but the facts and evidence tell me it is not."

President Ronald Reagan, March, 1987

A noteworthy blemish on the Reagan presidency is the *Iran/Contra* scandal. The United States had cut off diplomatic relations with Iran after the hostage crisis, and the *Boland Amendment* passed unanimously by Congress and signed by President Reagan in 1982 had explicitly forbidden funding the anticommunist *Contra* rebels in *Nicaragua*. In spite of these factors, National Security Council staff-member Colonel *Oliver North* and NSC directors *Robert McFarlane* and *John Poindexter* concocted a scheme to clandestinely sell missiles to Iran for use in its war against Iraq in exchange for Iranian assistance in freeing American hostages held by the *Hezbollah* terrorist group in Lebanon. The money from the missile sales was then funneled to the Contras for supplies. When a plane carrying supplies to the Contras was shot down, the scheme was revealed and numerous Reagan staffers were indicted and convicted. North famously shredded documents subpoenaed by Congress. President Reagan first denied knowledge of the illegal scheme, and then appeared out of touch and forgetful about whether he knew of it or not.

As President Reagan neared the end of his second term, the Iran/Contra affair would tarnish his reputation, implying that he was either willfully breaking the law or oblivious of those around him who were.

By the time Gorbachev
came along,
the Russian bear
wasn't quite so intimidating
as it had been during
Stalin's reign.

Mikhail Gorbachev was the last leader of the Soviet Union, serving as both General Secretary of the Communist Party and Soviet President. After living through Stalin's cruel tenure, Gorbachev envisioned a less totalitarian USSR. Upon taking office in 1985, Gorbachev would attempt to loosen restrictions both politically and economically. Gorbachev's policy of *"glasnost"* allowed for greater freedom of expression, while his policy of *"perestroika"* called for a restructuring of the economy that would allow some private ownership of assets. Gorbachev would end the Soviet Union's disastrous war in Afghanistan and attempt negotiations to slow the arms race with the United States. Most significantly, when the other eastern bloc nations of the *Warsaw Pact* began to abandon communism, Gorbachev did nothing to stop them, as opposed to previous attempted changes in Hungary, East Germany & Czechoslovakia many years earlier. In 1991, an attempted coup against Gorbachev by the Soviet military would fail, but Gorbachev would be replaced as the leader of a now independent Russia by *Boris Yeltsin*.

It really wound up rather a more tepid war, no ?

A great triumph for the foreign policies of President Reagan and President *George H. W. Bush* who would succeed him was the end of the Cold War. Starting in *Poland* in 1989, an anti-communist uprising led by *Lech Walesa* and the *Solidarity* labor union would upend the eastern bloc, and a peaceful democratic surge would course through eastern Europe, toppling governments from the Baltic to the Adriatic and replacing them with popularly-elected non-communist alternatives. Even the symbol of division between east and west, the Berlin Wall, would topple in 1989, with East and West Germany reunifying shortly thereafter.
By 1991, the Soviet Union itself would collapse into 17 independent nations, and the pervasive fear of an imminent World War III receded from the minds of people all over the world.

The Iraqi Army was surrendering faster than we could capture them.

Perhaps "Desert Storm" was a little hyperbolic?

"Desert Shower?" "Desert Mist?"

I suppose they just don't have quite the same ring to them, do they?

August, 1990 would see *Iraq*, fresh off its war with Iran, invade the neighboring oil-rich nation of *Kuwait*. Iraqi dictator *Saddam Hussein* claimed that Kuwait was actually Iraq's 17th province, illegally separated from it by the British years earlier, and further that the Kuwaitis had been "slant-drilling" and stealing Iraqi oil. Possessing the fourth-largest military in the world, Iraq quickly toppled the Kuwaiti government, bringing the world's largest oil reserves in Saudi Arabia within easy reach.

President Bush assembled a coalition of 29 nations including Arab and Muslim states to liberate Kuwait, and in January of 1991 *Operation Desert Storm* commenced.

The American-led alliance used technological and military superiority to overwhelm the Iraqi forces holding Kuwait, securing Kuwait's freedom after 100 hours of merciless pounding from the air. Fearful of losing the support of his Arab and Muslim allies, President Bush declined to pursue the war beyond the Kuwaiti border, leaving Saddam Hussein in power, a decision that would later lead to an eventual invasion of Iraq by the president's son, President *George W. Bush*, in 2003.

Isn't it weird to think that only 30 years ago
we could be sufficiently shocked that a politician had lied to us
that it would negatively impact them at the voting booth?

Times sure have changed.

Although President Bush's popularity would soar with the success of the war against Iraq, he would quickly find himself in political jeopardy. During the 1988 election, President Bush had famously declared *"read my lips; no new taxes"* when queried about his budget plans. In spite of this, due to a ballooning federal deficit and a mild recession, in 1990 Bush would sign into law tax increases totaling $133,000,000,000. Conservative voters felt betrayed, and in 1992 Bush would lose his bid for re-election to Democrat *Bill Clinton*. Clinton's focus on the economy and the serious threat of independent billionaire *Ross Perot* who earned 19% of the popular vote would doom Bush's quest for a second term. Clinton would be the first "baby-boomer" president, and in spite of several serious personal indiscretions that would lead to his impeachment, the United States would flourish during the Clinton era, actually running a $63,000,000,000 budget surplus during Clinton's two terms, and the nation would know both peace and prosperity over his eight years in office.

"Is it a contract <u>with</u> America,
or a contract <u>on</u> America?"

The 1994 midterm elections would strike a decisive blow against the Clinton presidency as the Republicans took back both houses of Congress for the first time since 1954. Speaker of the House *Newt Gingrich* led the Republican wave by promoting a 14-point *"Contract with America"* that pledged to reduce taxes, decrease the size and influence of the federal government, and legislate against liberal policies such as gun control and abortion. The Republicans would live up to their pledge to introduce bills addressing these issues in Congress, but between presidential vetoes, Senate filibusters and the Supreme Court declaring some of the legislation unconstitutional, the goals of the Republicans were overwhelmingly rejected. Nonetheless, Republican control of Congress would serve as an impediment to many Democratic policy initiatives, but with a surging economy and the nation at peace, President Clinton would be re-elected fairly easily in 1996. The *hyper-partisanship* of the era, however, would linger to the present day and contribute to much of the nation's fractiousness that has made governing so challenging over the last 30 years.

"*Do you solemnly swear to tell the truth, the whole truth,*
& nothing but the truth, so help you God?"

"*Maybe we should just leave God out of this;*
the big guy has a lot on his mind,
and he wouldn't be interested in something trivial like this, would he?"

"*After all, Hilary's not making a big deal out of this;*
why should Congress?"

Without question, the low point of Bill Clinton's presidency was his impeachment in 1999 for an extramarital affair he had conducted with White House intern *Monica Lewinsky*. Allegations of Clinton's infidelity had hounded him since he was Governor of Arkansas, but in 1998 investigations into possible crimes committed by the Clintons while in Arkansas regarding the *Whitewater* real estate development conducted by Special Prosecutor *Ken Starr* revealed Clinton's indiscretions with Lewinsky. Although the Whitewater suspicions did not lead to indictments, Starr presented illegally taped phone calls from government employee *Linda Tripp* that not only revealed the affair, but also the existence of DNA evidence on a dress Lewinsky had worn while involved with the President. Clinton had testified under oath that he *"did not have sexual relations with that woman,"* and when the evidence to the contrary was revealed, Clinton became the second president ever to be impeached. Clinton would be acquitted, largely along partisan lines, on charges of perjury and obstruction of justice, but it became clear to all that Clinton was not only an adulterer, but a liar as well.

"If they can't even run an election competently,
how can we expect them to run the country?"

The election of 2000 would be the closest since 1876, and, like that election, would only be resolved by extraordinary measures. Democratic Vice President *Al Gore* earned 500,000 more popular votes than Republican Governor *George W. Bush* of Texas, but the electoral tally was so close that the votes of Florida would determine the outcome. With a disparity of only 537 votes out of millions cast, and a contentious recount run under the authority of Governor *Jeb Bush*, George Bush's brother and further marred by allegations of confusing ballots and *"dimpled chads"* which prevented scanning machines from processing them correctly, the nation waited with baited breath for a resolution to become evident. Eventually, when Bush appealed to the Supreme Court for a decision on the recount, a 5-4 decision in *Bush v. Gore*, with all five Republican-nominated justices deciding for Bush and all four Democrat-nominated justices deciding for Gore, George W. Bush was elected President of the United States.

*"One of the worst days in American history
saw some of the bravest acts in American history.
We'll always honor the heroes of 9/11.
Here at this hallowed place,
we pledge that we will never forget their sacrifice."*
President George W. Bush

On *September 11th, 2001*, the United States suffered the worst attack ever by a foreign power on US soil when *Al-Qaeda* terrorists commandeered three passenger jets and flew them into the World Trade Center and the Pentagon. A fourth plane, *United Flight 93*, would crash into a field in Shanksville, Pennsylvania after the passengers fought back against the terrorists. Nearly 3,000 Americans would be killed and the nation unified in its desire for justice and retribution. When the *Taliban* government of *Afghanistan* refused to turn over *Osama bin-Laden* and other Al-Qaeda leaders, the US invaded Afghanistan and toppled the Taliban regime. As a consequence of this, the US would find itself embroiled in its longest war ever, culminating only 20 years later when President *Joe Biden* would withdraw US forces from Afghanistan. In 2003, President Bush would claim a link existed between Al-Qaeda and Iraq. The Bush administration would also claim that Iraq was in possession of *weapons of mass destruction*, in contravention of an agreement negotiated with the United Nations. Although both of these claims would prove false, in 2003 the United States invaded Iraq and toppled Saddam Hussein in *Operation Iraqi Freedom*. The US would remain enmeshed in Iraq for almost two decades, and the cost of these two long wars would include 900,000 lives, 15,000 of which were American servicemen or contractors, while the cost to American taxpayers would reach $8,000,000,000,000.

"Was the first President Bush really so great that we needed a sequel?"

"Did we learn nothing from the Adams presidencies?"

The booming economy of the late 1990's would come crashing to a halt by 2002. The *"dot.com"* technology bubble collapsed, with the value of the stock market crashing by 38%. President Bush had implemented a $1,350,000,000 tax cut, with nearly all of the benefits going to the top 5% of earners. The tax cuts and stock market collapse coupled with fighting two wars concurrently would double the national debt from five to ten trillion dollars during Bush's two terms. Many investors, spooked by the stock market, had plunged their money into real estate, which thanks to poorly-regulated markets and shady business practices would also crash in 2008. leading to the *Great Recession*. during which the stock market would crash an additional 50%. Abandoning his supply-side trickle-down economic policies, President Bush would establish the *Troubled Asset Relief Program* which disbursed $700,000,000,000 to banks and companies deemed *"too big to fail."* Although President Bush had won re-election against Senator *John Kerry* in 2004 on a campaign of *"family values"* which demonized gay marriage and slandered Bronze Star Vietnam veteran Kerry as unpatriotic, between the economy, the two wars which had seemingly no end in sight, and a bungled response to *Hurricane Katrina*, by the end of his second term President Bush was highly unpopular with Democrats and Republicans alike, and his poor performance would set the stage for a transformative election that many Americans could not have dreamt possible.

Rosa sat
so that Martin could march
so that Barack could run.

If you don't know what I'm talking about,
then you clearly skipped several earlier pages
to find out how this whole story ends.

Get back about 80 pages
and learn what you were supposed to.

Go ahead; I'll wait.

When Senator *Barack Obama* defeated Republican
John McCain in the 2008 presidential election,
the United States for the first time in its 220 year history
elected an African American president. While young and
relatively inexperienced as a politician, President Obama was
greeted by many as a refreshing alternative to what had
become an exceedingly unpopular Republican political
establishment. Democrats would gain control of not only the
White House but of both houses of Congress as well. The fact
that America could overcome the clear and pervasive racism of
its past inspired many that true change and reform
was possible. While incessant partisan obstructionism would
keep Obama from achieving many of his goals,
for a majority of Americans his election was indeed
an encouraging sign of hope.

Several consecutive administrations were right on top of immigration reform.

While Americans seem proud to celebrate that we are a nation of immigrants, the willingness of many Americans to welcome additional immigrants has been quite conflicted for many years. The *Immigration & Nationality Act* of 1965 eliminated quotas tied to ethnicity and instead emphasized relation to US citizens and immigrants with desirable job skills. Lax enforcement of border crossings led to a significant influx of migrant workers who filled millions of jobs for meager wages that Americans were not willing to do. The Reagan administration granted amnesty to over 3,000,000 undocumented migrants, while both the Clinton and Bush administrations alike did little to address the immigration issue. In 2012, President Barack Obama would implement the *Deferred Action for Childhood Arrivals* Act which protected children already in the United States from deportation. President Donald Trump would campaign on a virulently anti-immigration platform opposing DACA, demanding that Mexico build a wall along the 2,000 mile southern border and pledging to cut down on immigration in general, including even asylum-seekers and refugees fleeing violence and repression.

"Oh don't be absurd;
there are all kinds of tea parties that cater to
outside-the-box thinkers such as myself."

Leading the opposition to Obama's agenda was the newly-formed *Tea Party* coalition of conservatives and libertarians. The Tea Party would come to comprise approximately 20% of the electorate, and would wield their influence to steer the Republican Party even more to the right on issues ranging from abortion to taxes to government regulation to gun control to immigration. The Republicans would regain control of the House of Representatives in the 2010 midterm elections and the Tea Party would evolve into the *America First/Make America Great Again* core that would help to elect *Donald Trump* in 2016, and which would form the hard-core conspiracy-driven base that would attack the Capitol on *January 6th, 2021.*

"We're doing our best to maintain the vital signs…"

"Of the patient, or of the legislation?"

The signature accomplishment of the Obama administration
was the *Affordable Care Act* of 2010.
Against overwhelming Republican opposition, *"Obamacare"*
would extend health coverage to over 20,000,000 Americans
who otherwise could not attain it. The ACA prevented
insurers from denying coverage to those with pre-existing
conditions and allowed children to stay on their parents'
insurance until the age of 26. Over the next decade,
Republicans would try more than 50 times to dismantle
or defund the ACA, but it has remained in place and has added
a significant dimension of security and well-being
to the lives of millions of American families,
joining Social Security, Medicare & Medicaid
as backstops guaranteeing the American dream
is accessible to all Americans.

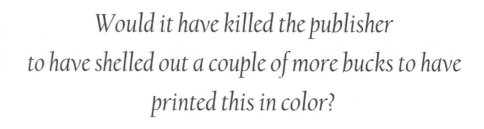

Would it have killed the publisher
to have shelled out a couple of more bucks to have
printed this in color?

This flag doesn't even show
a single color of the rainbow,
let alone all of them.

Cheapskates.

A mere 11 years after opposition to gay marriage
swung the 2004 presidential election
to Republican George W. Bush,
the Supreme Court made the most significant change
to LGBTQ+ rights in US history.
The 2015 5-4 ruling in *Obergefell v. Hodges*
declared same-sex marriage protected
under the 14th Amendment's right to privacy clause.
Although 36 states, the District of Columbia and Guam
had already conveyed some degree of legal status
to same-sex couples, the Court's ruling made it
indisputably the law of the land,
removing the government's influence
from a person's decision regarding
whom to love and build a life alongside.

You're not a victim for sharing your story.
You are a survivor setting the world on fire with your truth.
And you never know who needs your light, your warmth and raging courage.

Alexandra Elle

The *#Me Too movement* started in 2006
when *Tarana Burke* came forward with her story of having
survived sexual abuse as a child. The movement raised
awareness of sexual assault and harassment against women
and sought to empower victims by exposing harassers
and demanding consequences for men who had abused
their positions of power for their benefit.
An emphasis on victim empowerment and denial of complicity
led many women to come forward, with the movement gaining
widespread attention in 2017 when prominent celebrities were
the target of allegations, most notably movie producer
Harvey Weinstein and actor/comedian *Bill Cosby*,
who would both be sentenced to lengthy prison sentences.
While women still are subject to gender-based discrimination
and sexual harassment and assault, the greater attention
generated in recent years has shined a spotlight
on the need for these issues to be continually addressed.

No matter how big a nation is, it is no stronger than its weakest people,
and as long as you keep a person down,
some part of you has to be down there to hold him down,
so it means you cannot soar as you might otherwise.

Marian Anderson

The *Black Lives Matter* movement began in July 2013 after the acquittal of *George Zimmerman* in the shooting death of African-American teen *Trayvon Martin* in 2012. The movement became nationally recognized for street demonstrations that followed the 2014 deaths of *Michael Brown* who was killed by police in Ferguson, Missouri and *Eric Garner* who was killed by police in New York City. The death of *George Floyd* in Minneapolis in 2020 would lead to the conviction of four police officers found complicit in his murder. The decentralized movement was regarded as controversial by some Americans who felt it unfairly targeted good police officers along with bad, and that it ignored the desire of many African-Americans to have a strong police presence in Black communities. Nonetheless, the overwhelming disparity in deaths and arrests between Black and White Americans posed a problem that continues to demand attention. *"Defund the Police"* movements rose and fell in popularity, with new policies having failed thus far to quell crime rates in the United States.

"Cut him some slack;

It's not like he doesn't have a lot on his mind…"

The 2016 presidential election would feature possibly the two least-appealing candidates in US history. TV personality and alleged business tycoon *Donald Trump* surprised the Republican establishment by winning the Republican primary, while former First Lady, Senator & Secretary of State *Hilary Rodham Clinton* was the Democratic candidate. Clinton was the first female to ever head a major-party ticket, but her association with her husband's administration as well as an aloof, calculating personality turned off many voters, while even more were repelled by Trump's blatant bigotry, misogyny and well-documented history of lying and cheating business partners. Overcoming numerous documented instances of Trump's lack of any moral values whatsoever, the acknowledged adulterer and thrice-married Trump earned the support of fundamentalist Christians at the same time that the "billionaire" earned the votes of disaffected working-class Americans. Clinton would earn 2.864,985 more popular votes than Trump, but he would win the electoral college and become the 45th President of the United States, promising to *"make America great again."* Trump would give a massive tax cut to the wealthiest Americans and increase the national debt from $19 trillion to $28 trillion in four years after having promised to erase the debt in eight years. Trump would also pull the nation out of the *Paris Climate Accords* and the agreement designed to prevent Iran from acquiring a nuclear weapon while he instead pursued a xenophobic *"America First"* agenda.

"It's going to be a big, beautiful wall …
And Mexico is going to pay for it!"

"Problem solved."

As a candidate in the 2016 election, Donald Trump demonized illegal immigrants and catalyzed voters by pledging to erect a ***2,000 mile-long wall*** along the US-Mexico border. Moreover, Trump pledged that he would make Mexico pay for the wall. Trump would end up building a mere 458 miles of wall, most of which was constructed where barriers had already existed. Mexico never contributed a penny toward the construction of the 18-30 foot tall barriers, which proved easy to scale with a $15 ladder and easy to cut through with a simple handyman's grinder. Trump would end up allocating $15,000,000,000 of taxpayer money toward construction of the wall, most of it taken away from funds allocated by Congress to the Defense Department to provide for the men and women of the US military. $2,200,000,000 would be returned to the troops once President Biden took office. Migrants who continued to seek refuge or opportunity in the United States were treated with great hostility under President Trump's orders, with hundreds of children being separated from their families.

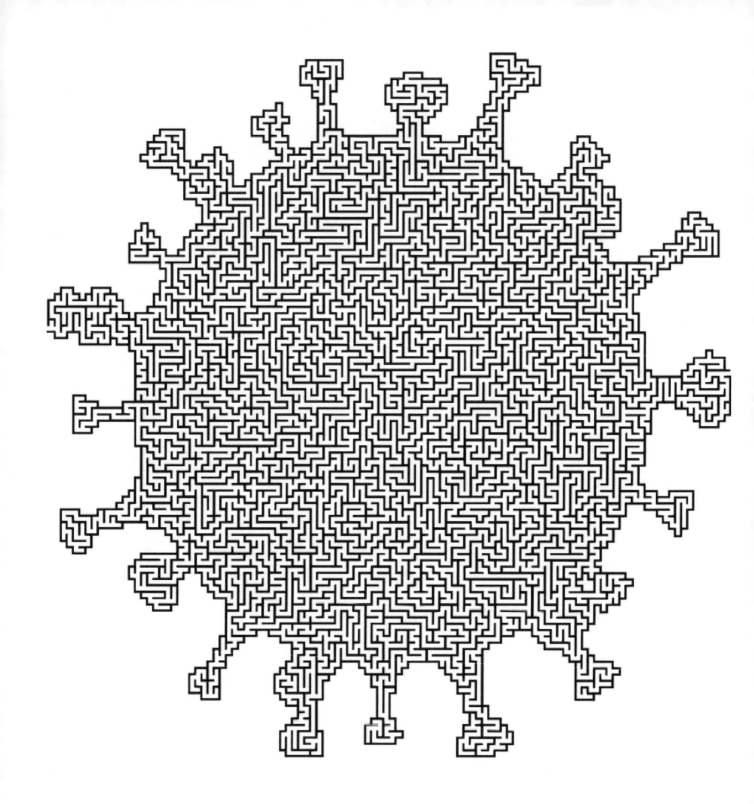

"Maybe bleach? Or a bright light?"

Early in 2020, both the United States and the world would face an enemy that would rival the Spanish Flu of a century prior. *COVID-19* would emerge and quickly force masking, quarantines, social distancing and most tragically, millions of cases of pulmonary illness that would take the lives of over 900,000 Americans and millions more worldwide as of early 2022. Hospitals would be overwhelmed as shortages of ventilators and personal protective equipment pushed the nation's health-care system to the brink. Miraculously, three vaccines would be developed in record time which dramatically reduced the severity of the illness and the likelihood of fatalities. Distribution of the vaccine would initially be slow and difficult, but by spring of 2021 any adult who wanted a vaccine could access it. Unfortunately, even though President Trump facilitated the creation of the vaccine, a striking number of his followers refused to take it, jeopardizing their fellow Americans and preventing the nation from achieving herd immunity. Unfounded fears of microchips and magnetization would emerge from the *Q-Anon* conspiracy adherents who believed that cannibalistic Democratic Satan-worshiping pedophiles introduced the virus so that the vaccine could corrupt Americans and cow them into submission.
I realize that if you believe this nonsense and have read this far in this book, you will reject everything I just wrote, but that is unlikely because this book uses multiple polysyllabic words that would have tripped you up and made you give up prior to now.

In 2017, Special Prosecutor *Robert Mueller* would conclude an investigation into Russian interference in the 2016 election. Mueller's investigation would lead to 34 indictments against Trump staffers and eight convictions. However, Mueller did not feel that he could constitutionally bring an indictment against a sitting president. When Democrats regained control of the House of Representatives after a sweeping victory in the midterm elections, President Trump was impeached for obstruction of Congress and abuse of power for having withheld $435,000,000 in military aid to American-ally Ukraine, suggesting that it would be released if Ukraine provided damaging information about

Vice President and Democratic presidential candidate *Joe Biden's* son. Trump would be acquitted along a near party-line vote in the Senate. Unlike the two presidents who had been impeached previously, Trump would subsequently be impeached a second time for encouraging the insurrection on *January 6th, 2021* that would take seven lives, lead to hundreds of prosecutions and convictions, and threaten the peaceful transition of power that had characterized every single presidential election in previous US history. A majority of 57 Senators, including seven Republicans would vote to convict Trump, but the needed $^2/_3$ majority was not reached, with several Republicans declining to convict because Trump was no longer a sitting president.
Regardless of what he says on the matter.

"…and after that,
the civil discourse pretty much deteriorated."

The 2020 election was perhaps the most contentious in US history. Although *Joe Biden* would defeat President Trump by exactly the same electoral margin of 306-232 that Trump had defeated Hilary Clinton, Biden would receive 7,052,770 more popular votes than Trump. All of this notwithstanding, Trump could not countenance the thought that he could lose and lobbed accusations of fraudulent elections and insisted that Vice President *Mike Pence* should refuse to certify the election. Over 60 court cases unanimously determined that there was no fraud, but Trump would continue to stoke suspicion and hatred among his followers. These same followers would be urged on by Trump on *January 6th, 2021* to attack the US Capitol in a manner that hadn't happened since the British attack in 1814 while we were at war. The nation watched aghast as insurrectionists attacked police officers and desecrated the Capitol. Biden would take over a nation wracked by a pandemic, a faltering economy, environmental crisis and an unending war in Afghanistan. During his first year in office, President Biden would struggle to bring *inflation* under control, with it reaching a 40-year high. Biden would manage to pass a multi-trillion dollar *infrastructure* bill to spur jobs and rebuild roads, bridges and electrical grids, and would strive to make our nation more energy-independent and environmentally responsible. Republican congressional opposition and a razor-thin majority in the Senate would prevent Biden from accomplishing much of his agenda.

There is so much more
to America's story
than what is written here.
Remember that everything
you do will be the subject of
another book chronicling
the years when you can
make a difference.
Please make sure that we all
will have a happy ending.

Made in the USA
Monee, IL
14 September 2022